COOKING FOR
ONE

CIDER MILL PRESS

BOOK PUBLISHERS

KENNEBUNKPORT, MAINE

13-Digit ISBN: 978-1-60433-813-3
10-Digit ISBN: 1-60433-813-X

This book may be ordered by mail from the publisher.
Please include $5.99 for postage and handling.
Please support your local bookseller first!

Books published by Cider Mill Press Book Publishers are available at special discounts for bulk purchases in the United States by corporations, institutions, and other organizations.
For more information, please contact the publisher.

Cider Mill Press Book Publishers
"Where good books are ready for press"
PO Box 454
12 Spring Street
Kennebunkport, Maine 04046

Visit us online!
cidermillpress.com

Typography: Bell MT and Gotham
Image Credits: All photography courtesy of Shutterstock

Printed in China
1 2 3 4 5 6 7 8 9 0
First Edition

TABLE OF CONTENTS

— INTRODUCTION —

There is something both wonderful and gratifying about cooking a meal for yourself. It takes time to thoughtfully choose a recipe, shop for the perfect ingredients, and prepare them correctly. In some way, the act of cooking could be considered the ultimate indulgence.

But cooking for one means different things to different people. For some, it's a chance to relax on a night when the entire family is booked with other activities, and they can bask in the quiet of an ordinarily bustling kitchen. For others, it's an opportunity to make a particular recipe that only appeals to them—and savor the outcome one bite at a time. And, for many, it is simply about acting out a routine and preparing their lunch, a simple dinner, or a quick snack.

If you can think of cooking as a comforting ritual, like preparing your morning coffee or tea, you'll start to view cooking for yourself as an enriching activity. Cooking for yourself, and enjoying specific recipes and meals, can create that same feeling of continuity, consistency, and care. With a bit of time, it'll help you shift from the anxiety and expectations that come with cooking for a crowd, and transform your kitchen into a celebratory space.

So often when we find ourselves alone, cooking an entire meal seems a bit much, and out comes the box of cereal or a takeout menu. But, if you can learn to purchase the right amount of ingredients and prepare them ahead of time, you'll find yourself sharpening your chef's knife more often than not.

This book intends to teach you how to master that planning and preparing, so that you can make those solitary nights something to look forward to. By teaching you how to shop, cut back on waste, store food properly, and by introducing you to a number of delicious recipes, the hope is that you'll come to a place where the pleasure you get from cooking for yourself trumps the ease of pouring cereal into a bowl.

CHAPTER ONE

Tips and Techniques

Preparing your kitchen, fridge, and pantry for cooking solo is a giant first step toward creating great meals when you're on your own. The right tools, kitchen gadgets, utensils, and cookware make navigating the kitchen on your own a lot easier, especially if everything is organized and easy to access. Stocking your fridge, freezer, and cabinets with the right staples makes cooking a real pleasure, and it cuts down on food waste tremendously. So dive in, and transform your nights at home alone into something to enjoy.

HANDY TOOLS AND GADGETS

CHEF'S KNIFE: Having a good one of these makes preparation a cinch, and, as it can perform any function you may need, simplifies things quite a bit. Some tried-and-true brands are Wusthof, Shun, and J.A. Henckels, while the Victorinox Fibrox provides the best bang for your buck.

A DOUBLE-LAYER STEAMER: Two layers make it possible to steam protein and vegetables, or any combination of ingredients, at once. A good one of these also makes it easy to measure out enough materials for just one. Joyce Chen offers a simple bamboo version that is solid, and Black & Decker also produces a quality offering.

SALAD SPINNER: It may seem like a luxury, but washing and spinning lettuce for an entire week saves both time and money, making this a necessity. A large amount of lettuce, spun, dried, and then packed properly with paper towels (or clean dishcloths) and stored in a container with a lid or a Ziploc bag will make it easy, and inviting, to whip up salads all week long.

SMALL SAUCEPAN AND FRYING PAN: As you'll be preparing small, simple meals, a quality one of these is essential. A good, small cast-iron frying pan is a good investment, as it will last forever, and cleaning it is a cinch.

SMALL BAKING DISH: Anything that is going in the oven—a stuffed vegetable, baked pasta, or lasagna—will want to be cooked in this. The small baking dish is also good for reheating leftovers.

SMALL STORAGE CONTAINERS: Either glass or plastic, with lids. Keep them organized in a cupboard so that they are easy to grab. They help immensely with storage, meal planning, and preparation.

ICE CUBE TRAYS: Since you'll be using a lot less of things, you'll want a few of these to help store broth, sauces, and frozen herbs. Use them wisely, and you'll always have accurately measured recipe ingredients that are ready to go.

MORTAR AND PESTLE: The classic mortar and pestle has been used in food preparation around the world since ancient times, and is indispensable for making single-serving recipes. It is easy to store, it's simple to use, and it's quick to clean, unlike the more modern mini food processor.

IMMERSION BLENDER: This is perfect for getting your soups and sauces to the desired consistency. Not only that, it is easy to clean.

STOCKING THE FRIDGE AND FREEZER

When you're cooking for yourself, it's always a good idea to scale down and purchase less, which makes storage key. It's less expensive to purchase a family pack of chicken or pork chops and divide them into separate freezer bags or freezer-friendly containers.

Fresh herbs can be grown on a windowsill or outdoors in the summer, making it easy to snip off exactly what you need, and ensuring that you're always using fresh ingredients. If you don't have a green thumb and are going to purchase herbs at the market, you can often buy them in small amounts. If you're going to go this route, refrigerate them in water and cover the container with a plastic bag. This permits them to last a week or two longer than if they are just tossed in the refrigerator drawer.

Broths and sauces can be parceled out easily into one-cup servings, and then frozen. This cuts down on waste, and simplifies your preparation. To do this, fill a muffin tin with a broth or sauce and put it in the freezer. When frozen, you'll have a dozen half-cup blocks that can be stored in a freezer bag. And don't worry about running out of space—these broth bags can be stacked on top of one another. Just make sure to label each one so that you know what you're grabbing, and what you're running low on.

Sure, the small containers of milk and cheese, and a half-dozen eggs are more expensive, but you'll waste a lot less. Search out the single-serving sizes for dairy products like cottage cheese, sour cream, and yogurt. Don't be afraid to go small with these staples.

These days, a variety of rice and grains are available in two-serving-sized frozen pouches. Pop one of these into the microwave and you're halfway to two nights of delicious meals. If you're interested in testing these out, Trader Joe's and Uncle Ben's are brands that can be trusted.

STOCKING THE PANTRY

Spices and dried herbs can be purchased in the bulk section of your supermarket, making it easy to buy small amounts. Resist the hesitation to load up and instead replenish your stores often, as you don't want these ingredients to grow stale.

Chicken and tuna come in one-serving cans. These can come in handy if you're in a hurry and need some protein, so make sure to keep a couple cans around.

Pasta, purchased by the pound, can be divided easily into three or four single-serving-sized bundles. Store these in bags or containers, and make your pasta preparation foolproof.

Keep plenty of rice and grains around. Storing them in mason jars, which include measurement markings on the side, makes it easy to see how much of a particular grain you'll need.

Tomato sauce, canned tomatoes, and tomato paste come in small-portion sizes. It's nice to have a variety in the pantry, so you can grab and go. Tomato paste also comes in tubes that can be refrigerated, and will last a little bit longer than their canned brethren.

Search out the smallest possible jars of condiments like ketchup, mustard, mayonnaise, pesto, and olive tapenade. This will help you cut down on waste, and guarantee that you're using ingredients that haven't wandered well past their expiration dates.

CHAPTER TWO

Soups and Salads

Think one bowl and done.

When we make soup, the first thing that comes to mind is a giant pot and a ladle. Most recipes are intended to make large amounts, which is perfect when there are 10 people sitting around the table. But most of the time, that soup hangs around for days, taking up too much room in the fridge. Typically, by the third bowl, it's the last thing you want to see and it's time to think about something different. Similarly, making a single salad at home often leaves you with partial heads of lettuce and lots of stray vegetables. By thinking about a salad in advance—purchasing the right amount of ingredients and learning how to store those components properly—it becomes more likely that you won't have to hit the salad bar. These nourishing soups and salads are perfect as a start to a meal or work great as a lighter main meal—a perfect one-serving course.

TIPS:

* Making small batches of soup calls for smaller amounts of broth. Freezing extra broth in a standard muffin pan will create 12 perfect half-cup discs that can be popped out once frozen and stored in a plastic bag. Just be sure to label the bags with what type of broth is inside so you don't get confused.

* The key to creating a fresh, interesting salad is having the right amount of ingredients and storing them properly. By purchasing a few different types of lettuce, washing and spinning it in advance,

and bagging single servings, it becomes a simple, easy-to-use base for all types of salads. Cleaning, cutting, preparing, and packaging fresh vegetables in advance creates an in-house salad bar for one, offering myriad options.

* Buying one bag or box of lettuce at the grocery store and then dividing it into smaller bags makes it simple to make one salad at a time. This also applies to pre-cut vegetables, which can be a time-saver.

BLACK BEAN SOUP

Black bean soup is nice on its own, or served with a variety of toppings. It can be as spicy as you desire. And, by using vegetable broth, it is perfect for vegetarians and vegans.

ACTIVE TIME 30 MINUTES

Ingredients

1 tablespoon olive oil

¼ cup onion, diced

¼ teaspoon ground cumin

⅛ teaspoon chili powder

⅛ teaspoon dried oregano

⅛ teaspoon hot pepper sauce

Salt and pepper to taste

½ bay leaf

1 cup chicken or vegetable broth

1 cup black beans, rinsed

½ cup tomato sauce [See recipe on page 125.]

Chopped cilantro leaves for garnish, optional

Greek yogurt for garnish, optional

Directions

Heat the olive oil in a small saucepan over medium-high heat. Add the onion, spices, hot pepper sauce, salt, and pepper. Stir occasionally until the onion has softened, about 10 minutes.

Stir in the bay leaf, broth, black beans, and tomato sauce. Feel free to add more broth, if necessary. Bring the soup to a rolling boil, then turn down the heat and allow the soup to simmer for 20 minutes.

Remove the soup from heat and puree (either in blender or in pan using immersion blender). Garnish with a dollop of yogurt and cilantro, if preferred, and serve.

HEARTY VEGETABLE SOUP WITH PISTOU

The fresher the vegetables in this soup, the better. Similar to pesto, pistou originates from the south of France and is an olive oil-based sauce, which adds a zesty flavor.

ACTIVE TIME 35 MINUTES

Ingredients

Soup:

1 tablespoon olive oil

¼ small onion, chopped

½ celery stalk, chopped

½ carrot, chopped

1 small zucchini, chopped (about ½ cup)

1 handful of green beans, chopped

1 handful of cherry tomatoes, quartered

1 handful of baby potatoes, quartered

2 cups chicken or vegetable broth

1 bay leaf

Salt and pepper to taste

Pistou:

1 garlic clove

Kosher salt to taste

¼ cup basil leaves, torn

3 to 4 cherry tomatoes, diced

A splash of olive oil

2 tablespoons gouda, grated

(continued on next page)

Directions

Heat olive oil in a small saucepan over medium-high heat. Add the onion, celery, carrot, and a pinch of salt. Stir occasionally and cook until the vegetables are softened, about 10 minutes.

Stir in the broth and the bay leaf, which should gently cover the vegetables. Feel free to add more broth, if necessary. Bring the soup to a rolling boil, then turn down the heat so that the soup simmers.

Add the remaining vegetables to the soup and continue to simmer.

While the soup is simmering, gather the ingredients for the pistou. Crush the clove of garlic, kosher salt, basil leaves, and cherry tomatoes together with a mortar and pestle. Add the grated gouda, stir to combine, and set aside.

When the vegetables in the soup have softened, pour into a bowl, and top with the fresh pistou.

LAMB MEATBALL SOUP

As the name suggests, the lamb meatballs are the stars of this soup, as they impart a lovely flavor to the broth.

ACTIVE TIME 40 MINUTES

Ingredients

Meatballs:

2 small green onions, diced

¼ pound ground lamb

⅛ teaspoon salt

½ teaspoon ginger, minced

¼ teaspoon allspice

¼ teaspoon cumin

1 tablespoon mayonnaise

2 tablespoons bread crumbs

Soup:

1 tablespoon olive oil

1 shallot, minced

2 garlic cloves, smashed

1½ cups chicken or vegetable broth

3 tablespoons crumbled feta for garnish

2 tablespoons freshly chopped mint leaves for garnish

Directions

Combine the green onions, ground lamb, salt, ginger, allspice, mayonnaise, and bread crumbs in a bowl and mix gently with your hands.

Use your hands or a small ice cream scoop to form meatballs from the contents of the bowl.

Heat olive oil in a small frying pan and add the meatballs, turning until brown.

Directions
(continued)

When the meatballs are brown all over, remove them from the frying pan and let them drain on a paper towel or brown bag.

Heat olive oil in a small saucepan over medium-high heat. Add the shallot and garlic. Stir occasionally and cook until they are softened, approximately 10 minutes.

Add the broth and the meatballs. Feel free to add more broth, if desired. Bring the soup to a rolling boil and then turn the heat down until the soup is simmering. Continue to cook for approximately 20 minutes.

Garnish with feta cheese and mint leaves, and serve.

WHITE BEAN, GARLIC, AND ROSEMARY SOUP

The richness of the white beans makes this soup a perfect dinner or hearty lunch. It can also be pureed for a creamier version.

ACTIVE TIME 35 MINUTES

Ingredients

1 tablespoon olive oil

1 garlic clove, smashed

½ celery stalk, diced

½ carrot, diced

¼ onion, diced

1 sprig rosemary, finely chopped

1 cup chicken or vegetable broth

1 cup white beans, drained and rinsed

Freshly chopped parsley for garnish

Freshly grated parmesan cheese for garnish

¼ cup chopped Swiss chard

Directions

Heat olive oil in a small saucepan over medium-high heat. Add the garlic, celery, carrot, and onion. Stir occasionally and cook until the vegetables have softened, about 10 minutes.

Stir in the broth, white beans, and Swiss chard. Add more broth, if necessary. Add the rosemary, bring the soup to a rolling boil, and then turn down the heat so that the soup simmers. Allow to simmer for approximately 20 minutes.

If you want a creamier version, use a blender or an immersion blender to puree the soup.

Garnish with parmesan cheese and parsley, and serve.

SPICY CARROT GINGER SOUP

This soup is particularly satisfying when it's cold or damp. The ginger creates a warmth that goes far beyond the actual temperature of the soup.

ACTIVE TIME 35 MINUTES

Ingredients

1 tablespoon olive oil

2 to 3 large shallots, chopped (approximately ¼ cup)

½ pound carrots, peeled and chopped (approximately 1¼ cup)

1 teaspoon ginger, minced

¼ teaspoon ground cumin

¼ teaspoon ground turmeric

⅛ teaspoon chili powder

1 cup chicken or vegetable broth

½ cup unsweetened coconut milk

Salt and pepper to taste

Chopped cilantro leaves for garnish, optional

Plain Greek yogurt for garnish, optional

Directions

Heat olive oil in a small saucepan over medium-high heat. Add the shallots, carrots, spices, and a pinch of salt. Stir occasionally and cook until the vegetables are softened, approximately 10 minutes.

Stir in the broth, which should cover the vegetables. Feel free to add more broth, if necessary. Bring the soup to a rolling boil and then turn down the heat so that the soup simmers. Continue cooking until the carrots are cooked through, approximately 10 minutes.

Directions
(continued)

Puree the soup using either a blender or an immersion blender. If a standard blender is used, return soup to pot.

Add the coconut milk, salt, and pepper.

Garnish with a dollop of yogurt and cilantro, if preferred, and serve.

CHICKEN CHILI

Instead of beef or turkey, this chili features grilled chicken.
Plus, the jalapeño pepper adds an extra kick.

Ingredients

1 tablespoon olive oil

¼ onion, chopped

1 garlic clove, smashed

¼ teaspoon ground cumin

¼ teaspoon cayenne pepper

⅛ teaspoon chili powder

½ teaspoon jalapeño pepper, diced

1½ cups fire roasted tomatoes, diced

Pinch of salt

1 cup kidney beans, rinsed

1 small chicken breast, grilled and chopped into bite-sized pieces

Avocados for garnish

Chopped cilantro leaves for garnish

Sour cream for garnish

Diced tomatoes for garnish

¼ cup fresh or frozen corn

Directions

Heat olive oil in a small saucepan over medium-high heat. Add the onion, garlic, spices, jalapeño pepper, and the pinch of salt. Stir occasionally and cook until the vegetables have softened, approximately 10 minutes.

Stir in the kidney beans, fire roasted tomatoes, and grilled chicken. Feel free to add more tomatoes, if desired. Add the corn, bring the soup to a rolling boil, and then turn down the heat so that the soup is simmering. Continue to cook for 20 minutes.

Garnish with sour cream, chopped cilantro, tomatoes, and avocados, and serve.

ONE-TOMATO SOUP

Whether you pick a tomato from your garden, choose one
at a local farmers market, or manage to find a delicious
vine-ripened variety at the grocery store, this soup focuses
on the beauty and flavor of one glorious tomato.

ACTIVE TIME 30 MINUTES

Ingredients

1 tablespoon olive oil

¼ small yellow onion, chopped

½ carrot, chopped

½ celery stalk, chopped

1 medium to large tomato,
peeled and chopped

1 tablespoon tomato paste

1½ cups chicken or vegetable
broth

Salt and pepper to taste

Directions

Heat olive oil in a small saucepan over medium-high heat.
Add the onion, carrot, and celery along with a pinch of salt.
Stir occasionally and cook until the vegetables are softened,
approximately 10 minutes.

Add the fresh tomato to the saucepan.

Add the broth, which should gently cover the tomato and
vegetables, and stir to combine. Feel free to add more broth, if
necessary. Bring the soup to a rolling boil and then turn down
the heat until the soup is simmering. Continue to cook until the
carrots are cooked through, approximately 10 minutes.

Directions
(continued)

Add tomato paste, salt, and pepper.

If you desire a more homogenous soup, use an immersion blender or standard blender to puree it, and serve.

Variation: For a creamier texture, add a splash of milk or cream to the soup. Coconut milk, almond milk, or other dairy alternatives also work well in this soup.

SALAD NICOISE

This traditional French salad makes any lunch or dinner feel like an escape. It is relatively easy to put together and feels like a novelty because it looks so beautiful when arranged on a plate.

ACTIVE TIME 30 MINUTES

Ingredients

2 tablespoons olive oil

1 tablespoon lemon juice

1 small shallot, minced

1 tablespoon fresh herbs (basil, thyme, oregano, or chives)

½ teaspoon Dijon mustard

Salt and pepper to taste

1 cup of mixed greens

½ can of solid tuna packed in oil (Italian varieties are preferable)

1 hardboiled egg, sliced

1 handful of new baby potatoes, cooked

1 handful of green beans, trimmed and blanched

1 handful of cherry tomatoes, quartered

½ small cucumber, diced

¼ cup black olives

Chopped parsley

Directions

Add the olive oil, Dijon mustard, lemon juice, shallot, and fresh herbs to a bowl and whisk until combined. Set bowl aside.

Arrange the mixed greens on a plate.

While the potatoes and green beans are still warm, toss them in the vinaigrette and place them on the bed of greens, making a nice, neat pile of each. Arrange the tuna on the plate.

Arrange the remaining vegetables, egg, olives, and parsley on the plate and serve.

CLASSIC SALAD LARDON

This is the perfect choice for an evening when you want a little more than just a salad. It not only tastes good, it looks great on a beautiful china plate next to a crisp glass of rosé.

ACTIVE TIME 20 MINUTES

Ingredients

3 tablespoons olive oil

2 tablespoons sherry wine vinegar

½ teaspoon Dijon mustard

Salt and pepper to taste

3 cups frisée greens

3 slices of bacon, cut into ½-inch pieces

1 tablespoon bacon grease, reserved from cooked bacon

½ cup croutons

1 egg, poached

Directions

Add olive oil, sherry wine vinegar, Dijon mustard, salt, and pepper to a small bowl, whisk until combined, and set aside.

Cook bacon in a frying pan over medium heat until golden brown. Remove from pan and drain on a brown paper bag or paper towel.

While bacon is cooling, add the frisée, bacon grease, and sherry vinaigrette to a bowl, and toss.

Add the pieces of bacon and the croutons to the bowl.

When salad is tossed with all the ingredients, poach an egg, place it in the center, and serve. For a poached egg with a runny center, crack one egg into a cup, drop it slowly into simmering water, and let it cook for approximately 2 minutes. Turn off heat, let the egg continue to cook for another 6 minutes in the simmering water, and then remove it with a slotted spoon.

CHOPPED SALAD

A chopped salad is a perfect meal, especially when
you have prepped the ingredients ahead of time.

ACTIVE TIME 20 MINUTES

Ingredients

2 tablespoons olive oil

1 tablespoon fresh lemon juice

1 garlic clove, diced

Salt and pepper to taste

3 cups of romaine hearts,
chopped

½ cucumber, chopped

1 handful of cherry tomatoes,
halved

3 tablespoons red onion, diced

1 tablespoon fresh chives,
chopped

1 cup chicken or turkey, diced

½ cup blue cheese, crumbled

Directions

Add the olive oil, lemon juice, garlic, salt, and pepper to a small
bowl, whisk until combined, and set aside.

Add the romaine hearts, cucumber, and cherry tomatoes to a larger
bowl and toss gently.

Sprinkle the red onion and chives on top of the vegetables and toss.

Add the cup of chicken or turkey and the crumbled blue cheese to
the vegetables and toss again. Add the dressing to the larger bowl
and toss until the components are evenly coated.

Directions
(continued)

Note: This salad can also be made in advance in a glass jar. Be sure to start with the dressing in the bottom of the jar, then add the onions and chives, followed by the turkey or chicken. Add the heavier vegetables in layers, with the hearts of romaine going on top.

KALE SALAD

This salad is perfect—hearty enough for dinner and many of the additional ingredients can be substituted, depending on what you have in your fridge.

ACTIVE TIME 20 MINUTES

Ingredients

2 tablespoons olive oil

1 tablespoon vinegar

1 garlic clove, diced

1 teaspoon mustard

Salt and pepper to taste

1 small bunch of kale, rinsed, ribs removed, and torn into bite-sized pieces (approximately 2 cups)

1 hardboiled egg, chopped

¼ cup sunflower seeds, toasted

¼ cup croutons

¼ cup parmesan cheese, grated

Directions

Add the olive oil, vinegar, garlic, mustard, salt, and pepper to a small bowl, whisk until combined, and set aside.

Add kale, hardboiled egg, sunflower seeds, bread crumbs, and parmesan cheese to a bowl, and toss.

Add the dressing to the bowl, toss again until combined, and serve.

AUTUMN ROAST ON A BED OF GREENS

This salad feels like autumn. Other fall vegetables can be substituted easily and you may find yourself making this every week during the season. It can be served chilled or at room temperature.

ACTIVE TIME 45 MINUTES

Ingredients

1 tablespoon olive oil for vinaigrette, and additional olive oil to coat roasted vegetables

1 tablespoon apple cider vinegar

1 teaspoon honey

1 teaspoon grainy mustard

Salt and pepper to taste

2 cups leafy greens

½ cup butternut squash, cubed

½ red onion, sliced

¼ cup dried cranberries

1 handful of walnuts

Directions

Add the olive oil, apple cider vinegar, honey, mustard, salt, and pepper to a small bowl, whisk until combined, and set aside.

Preheat oven to 400°.

Coat butternut squash and onions with olive oil, salt, and pepper, and spread evenly on a cookie sheet lined with parchment paper or foil. Place in oven and roast for a half-hour, or until golden brown.

Remove vegetables from the oven and allow to cool.

Directions
(continued)

Add the walnuts to a small frying pan and cook over medium heat until they are lightly browned. Remove walnuts from pan and let them cool.

When roasted vegetables and walnuts are cool, combine in a bowl with the cranberries and the vinaigrette, and toss.

Place the greens on a plate. Lay the dressed vegetables, walnuts, and cranberries over the bed of greens, and enjoy!

WILD RICE SALAD

Wild rice salad goes well with chicken and beef, but it can also be served over greens, or on its own as a snack. A rice cooker comes in handy when preparing this dish.

ACTIVE TIME 30 MINUTES **MAKES** 2 SERVINGS

Ingredients

Dressing:

2 tablespoons olive oil

¼ cup shallot, minced

2 tablespoons lemon juice

1 tablespoon honey

½ teaspoon salt

½ teaspoon apple cider vinegar

Salad:

¼ cup golden raisins

1 cup baby spinach, chopped

1 cup cooked wild rice

1 handful of toasted walnuts

¼ cup sauted mushrooms

¼ cup feta cheese

Directions

Dressing:

Add all of the ingredients to a small glass jar with a top. Shake well and set aside.

Salad:

Place the ingredients in a salad bowl and mix until well-combined.

Add dressing, toss until the contents of the bowl are evenly coated, and serve.

CHAPTER THREE

Meat

Meat is the star of every meal it appears in, whether you're cooking for a crowd, or just for yourself. Its flavor and versatility offer the opportunity to tailor it exactly to your tastes, and whip up something special in no time at all. Sure, a grilled rib eye seasoned with salt and pepper is delicious. But dress it up with a little béarnaise sauce and you'll turn your home into your own private bistro.

Same goes for a chicken breast, which can be prepared in countless ways depending on your whims and the season, and is perfect for a single person. The wonderful flavor of pork also provides a lot of options without a lot of effort on your behalf.

ONE FILET MIGNON AND THREE SAUCES

Filet mignon is a cut of beef taken from the small end of the tenderloin. But sometimes, big things come in small packages. Synonymous with special occasions, choosing this cut of meat is a great way to treat yourself when you're on your own. A 6 to 8 ounce filet is good for one person.

ACTIVE TIME 15 MINUTES

Ingredients

1 filet mignon, 6 to 8 ounces

1 tablespoon olive oil

Kosher salt and freshly ground pepper

Directions

Preheat oven to 425°. Remove the filet from the refrigerator and let it come to room temperature. This typically takes approximately 30 minutes. Season the top and bottom of the filet with the salt and pepper, gently pressing down on them so they adhere to the surface of the meat.

Place the olive oil in an oven-safe frying pan and cook over medium-high heat until it begins to sizzle. Add the filet to the pan and cook for 4 minutes. Do not touch the filet - you want it to sear really well on one side, as this will help keep the juices inside.

Directions
(continued)

After 4 minutes, use tongs to flip the filet over. Place the pan into the oven and cook for 6 to 7 minutes for medium rare.

When the filet is ready, remove it from the pan and let it rest for 10 minutes. Transfer it to a plate, and serve.

Filet mignon is special, but adding a sauce kicks it up another notch. Turn the page for three different options.

BÉARNAISE SAUCE

ACTIVE TIME 15 MINUTES

Ingredients

⅛ cup white wine

2 tablespoons white wine vinegar

3 teaspoons fresh tarragon, chopped

1 green onion, minced

¼ teaspoon black peppercorns

1 egg yolk

Salt to taste

3 tablespoons unsalted butter

Directions

Place the wine, vinegar, tarragon stems, green onion, and peppercorns in a small saucepan and simmer for 15 minutes. Strain the solids from the liquid and set aside.

Place the butter in a small saucepan and cook over medium heat while stirring constantly. When the butter stops foaming, transfer it to a small cup and set aside.

Place the wine-and-vinegar reduction, salt, and the egg yolk in a bowl, and combine with an immersion blender. When combined, slowly pour the melted butter into the bowl and continue blending until the sauce is creamy. Add the fresh tarragon and pour over your filet mignon.

MUSHROOM AND HERB SAUCE

ACTIVE TIME 15 MINUTES

Ingredients

3 tablespoons butter

1 tablespoon shallot, minced

1 garlic clove, minced

1 cup button mushrooms, sliced

1 tablespoon chives, chopped

1 teaspoon thyme leaves

1 tablespoon basil, chopped

1 tablespoon parsley, chopped

Salt and pepper to taste

Directions

Place the butter, shallot, and garlic in a frying pan and cook over medium heat until the butter is melted. Add the mushrooms and cook until soft.

Add the chives, thyme, basil, and parsley, stir until combined, and then pour over your filet mignon.

GREEN PEPPERCORN SAUCE

ACTIVE TIME 15 MINUTES

Ingredients

1 teaspoon olive oil

1 teaspoon shallot, minced

1 teaspoon green peppercorns packed in brine, smashed

1 tablespoon butter

1 teaspoon flour

1 tablespoon cognac

¼ cup beef broth

⅛ cup heavy cream

Salt and pepper to taste

Directions

Place the olive oil, shallot, green peppercorns, and butter in a frying pan and cook over medium heat until the shallot has softened. Remove the frying pan from the heat and add the cognac. Return to the burner and cook until the alcohol has burned off. Add the flour and cook for 1 minute.

Add beef broth and stir continuously for 3 minutes. Add the cream, stir until the sauce has been reduced by half, add the salt and pepper, and then pour over your filet mignon.

BEEF STEW

Beef stew is a hearty lunch or dinner, and
can be whipped up in no time at all.

ACTIVE TIME 25 MINUTES

Ingredients

1 pound stew beef

2 tablespoons olive oil

½ onion, chopped

1 celery stalk, chopped

1 garlic clove, minced

1 teaspoon flour

2 cups beef stock

1 bay leaf

½ cup carrots, sliced

½ cup baby potatoes, sliced in half

Salt and pepper to taste

Directions

Place half of the olive oil in a small Dutch oven and cook over medium-high heat until the oil begins to sizzle. Sprinkle salt and pepper over the stew beef and add it to the Dutch oven. Cook while turning the pieces of beef. When the beef is brown on all sides, remove and set aside.

Place the remaining olive oil in the Dutch oven and then add the celery and onion. Cook until soft, then add the flour and stir until it has dissolved. Add the beef stock and bay leaf, stir to combine, and then add the browned beef, carrots, and baby potatoes. Cook for 25 minutes, stirring occasionally.

When beef is tender, add additional salt and pepper, if necessary. Transfer stew to a bowl and serve.

BRAISED SHORT RIBS WITH RED WINE

A perfect recipe for a chilly night. This braise can be served over mashed potatoes, rice, or polenta.

ACTIVE TIME 20 MINUTES

Ingredients

1 pound bone-in short ribs (2 to 3 ribs)

1 teaspoon olive oil

Salt and pepper to taste

1 garlic clove, minced

1 shallot, minced

¼ cup carrot, diced

½ cup carrot, sliced

1 teaspoon tomato paste

½ cup beef stock

½ cup red wine

1 teaspoon brown sugar

Directions

Preheat your oven to 300°. While the oven is heating, place the olive oil in a small Dutch oven and cook over medium-high heat until the oil begins to sizzle. Sprinkle salt and pepper all over the short ribs and place them in the Dutch oven. Cook until they are browned on both sides, remove from the Dutch oven, and set aside.

Place the garlic, shallot, and carrots in the Dutch oven and cook until soft, approximately 3 to 5 minutes. Add the tomato paste, brown sugar, and wine and cook until the contents are bubbling.

Add the stock and return the short ribs to the pot. The short ribs should be covered in liquid; if not, add additional stock. Cover the Dutch oven and place it into the oven. Cook for one hour, or until meat is tender.

Directions
(continued)

Remove Dutch oven from the oven, and serve the short ribs over rice, mashed potatoes, or polenta.

One Chicken Breast and Six Ways to Make It

The simple chicken breast is an ideal protein for one person. All of these recipes go perfectly with a mixed green salad, or a vegetable, and maybe even potatoes or rice, depending on how hungry you are. And if you purchase a large bag of chicken breasts, pack them in individual freezer bags to make sure they don't go to waste.

CHICKEN BREAST WITH LEMON AND ROSEMARY

The piney rosemary and the brightness of lemon make a flavorful pairing in this recipe. This dish goes well with rice or mashed potatoes and a simple salad of mixed greens.

ACTIVE TIME 25 MINUTES

Ingredients

1 10-ounce chicken breast

1 tablespoon olive oil

1 garlic clove, minced

1 lemon

¼ cup white wine

1 tablespoon butter

2 small sprigs of rosemary

Salt and pepper to taste

Directions

Use a mallet to pound the chicken breast between two sheets of parchment paper or plastic wrap until ¼ inch thick.

Place the olive oil and garlic in a frying pan and cook over medium-high heat until the garlic softens. Place the chicken breast in the pan and cook on each side for 2 to 3 minutes, until each side is browned.

Cut the lemon in half. Squeeze the juice from one half into a bowl and set aside. Slice the other half and set aside.

Add the lemon juice, white wine, butter, and rosemary to the pan. Cook the chicken until the sauces in the pan begin to sizzle and chicken is cooked through.

Add the lemon slices, salt, and pepper, and serve.

CHICKEN BREAST WITH GREEN OLIVES, ALMONDS, AND CAPERS

The sauce produced with the olives, capers, and almonds make this chicken breast special—it is delicious served over wild rice.

ACTIVE TIME 30 MINUTES

Ingredients

1 10-ounce chicken breast

1 tablespoon olive oil

2 garlic cloves, sliced

½ cup green olives, pitted and sliced

2 tablespoons almonds, sliced

2 tablespoons capers

¼ cup white wine

Squeeze of fresh lemon

Salt and pepper to taste

1 cup wild rice, cooked

Directions

Use a mallet to pound the chicken breast between two sheets of parchment paper or plastic wrap until ¼ inch thick. Season both sides of the chicken with salt and pepper.

Place the olive oil and garlic in a frying pan and cook over medium-high heat until the garlic softens. Place the chicken breast in the pan and cook on each side for 5 to 6 minutes, until each side is browned.

Directions
(continued)

Add the white wine and continue to cook until it begins to bubble. Add the green olives, almonds, and capers, and cook until the sauce is heated through. Squeeze the lemon over the pan and then remove it from the heat.

Serve over the wild rice, making sure to spoon the sauce, olives, capers, and almonds over the chicken.

HERBED AND BREADED CHICKEN BREAST

Freshly made herbed bread crumbs make all the difference in this dish.

ACTIVE TIME 15 MINUTES

Ingredients

1 10-ounce chicken breast

1 tablespoon olive oil

1 tablespoon butter

1 garlic clove, minced

½ cup of fresh herbed bread crumbs

½ cup of flour

1 egg, beaten

Directions

Bread crumbs:

Place one piece of stale bread, salt and pepper to taste, ⅛ teaspoon garlic salt, ½ teaspoon basil, ½ teaspoon chive, ½ teaspoon parsley, and ½ teaspoon sage in a food processor and pulse until crumbs form. Transfer to a bowl and set aside.

Chicken:

Use a mallet to pound the chicken breast between two sheets of parchment paper or plastic wrap until ¼ inch thick. Pour the flour into a bowl and set aside. Dip the chicken into the beaten egg, into the flour, and then into the herbed bread crumbs.

Place the olive oil and garlic in a frying pan and cook over medium-high heat until the garlic softens. Place the chicken breast into the pan and cook on each side for 3 to 4 minutes, until the bread crumbs are crispy. When the chicken is cooked through, remove from the pan and serve with your favorite side.

STUFFED CHICKEN BREAST WITH SPINACH AND LEMON

Sweet ricotta, parmesan cheese, fresh baby spinach, and diced black olives create a light stuffing for this chicken breast. Topped by the resulting lemon-and-spinach sauce, it goes perfectly with mashed cauliflower.

ACTIVE TIME 20 MINUTES

Ingredients

1 10-ounce chicken breast

½ cup ricotta cheese

2 tablespoons parmesan cheese

1 cup fresh baby spinach, plus ¼ cup fresh baby spinach, chopped

¼ cup diced black olives

1 egg

Salt and pepper to taste

1 tablespoon olive oil

1 tablespoon butter

1 garlic clove

1 small shallot, minced

⅛ cup of fresh lemon juice

1 tablespoon of fresh lemon zest

¼ cup white wine

¼ cup chicken broth

Directions

Preheat oven to 350° and grease a small baking dish with olive oil.

Place the ricotta, parmesan, chopped baby spinach, olives, and egg in a bowl, stir until well-combined, and set aside.

Directions
(continued)

Slice the chicken breast along one side to create a pocket for the stuffing. Season with salt and pepper and fill the chicken breast with the stuffing, securing it with toothpicks if necessary.

Place the chicken in the baking dish and cook for 30 to 40 minutes, or until chicken is completely cooked through.

While the chicken is cooking, place the olive oil and butter in a frying pan and cook over medium-high heat until the butter melts. Add the garlic and shallot and cook until soft. Stir in the lemon juice, lemon zest, white wine, and chicken broth, and cook until the sauce is reduced by half. Add the remaining spinach and stir until wilted. Remove pan from heat and set aside.

Remove the chicken from the oven and place on a plate. Spoon the sauce in the pan over it, and serve with mashed cauliflower. (See next page.)

CAULIFLOWER MASH

A handful of cauliflower florets and a splash of broth make
a quick mash to go along with all sorts of dishes.

ACTIVE TIME 10 MINUTES

Ingredients

1 cup cauliflower florets

**½ cup stock, vegetable if you
would like this to be vegetarian**

1 garlic clove, minced

1 tablespoon olive oil

Salt and pepper to taste

Parsley for garnish

Directions

Place the olive oil and garlic in a small saucepan and warm
over medium-high heat.

Add stock and bring to a boil.

Add cauliflower florets and cover the saucepan.

Reduce heat to medium-low and continue to cook for 10 minutes,
or until cauliflower is soft.

Smash the cauliflower with potato masher until smooth.

Garnish with parsley, and serve.

PAN-FRIED CHICKEN BREAST WITH SAUSAGE GRAVY

This Southern favorite goes well with
mashed sweet potatoes and greens.

ACTIVE TIME 30 MINUTES

Ingredients

1 10-ounce chicken breast

1 tablespoon butter

1 sweet Italian sausage, casing removed

1 tablespoon flour

Salt and pepper to taste

Pinch of cayenne pepper

Pinch of dried mustard

¾ cup whole milk

2 tablespoons olive oil

1 egg, beaten

½ cup flour

½ cup fresh bread crumbs

Directions

Sausage gravy:

Place the butter in a small saucepan and cook over medium-high heat until it is melted. Add the sausage and cook for 5 minutes, or until it is broken up into small pieces and brown. Add the flour, salt, pepper, cayenne, and mustard, and stir until combined. When the mixture is heated through, add the milk and stir until mixture is creamy. Cover pan with a lid and set aside.

Directions
(continued)

For chicken:

Use a mallet to pound the chicken breast between two sheets of parchment paper or plastic wrap until ¼ inch thick.

Place the olive oil in a frying pan and cook over medium-high heat until the oil begins to sizzle. Dredge the chicken breast in the flour, egg, and bread crumbs, and place in pan. Cook, while turning, for 8 to 10 minutes, until the chicken is golden brown. Remove from pan and serve with the sausage gravy on top.

ROASTED CHICKEN BREAST WITH CHILI AND CORN SALSA

If you are fortunate enough to have fresh poblano peppers, you can drizzle them with olive oil, roast them, and include them in the salsa that tops this delicious chicken dinner. This dish is perfect with a mixed green salad.

ACTIVE TIME 20 MINUTES

Ingredients

1 10-ounce chicken breast

Salt and pepper to taste

2 tablespoons olive oil

⅛ teaspoon garlic powder

⅛ teaspoon chili powder

3 tablespoons poblano pepper, chopped (They come in a can, or you can roast fresh ones yourself.)

1 cup corn (frozen and thawed, or steamed and cut from cob will work)

⅓ cup red onion, diced

¼ cup cilantro, chopped

2 tablespoons lime juice

3 tablespoons red bell pepper, diced

¼ cup tomato, chopped

Directions

Preheat oven to 375° and grease a small baking dish with olive oil.

Place the garlic powder, chili powder, salt, and pepper in a small bowl and combine. Slather the chicken breast with the olive oil and then dip into the spice mix until coated.

When the oven is ready, place the chicken into the baking pan and bake for 20 to 30 minutes, until chicken is cooked through.

While the chicken is cooking, place the poblano pepper, corn, red onion, cilantro, lime juice, red pepper, tomato, salt, and pepper in a bowl, stir until well-combined, and set aside.

When chicken is cooked, remove pan from the oven, place the chicken breast on a plate, and top with the salsa. Serve with a mixed green salad.

BRAISED CHICKEN BREAST WITH CIDER VINEGAR

This braised chicken breast captures the flavors of the fall.
It goes well with couscous and a mixed green salad.

ACTIVE TIME 30 MINUTES

Ingredients

1 10-ounce chicken breast

1 tablespoon olive oil

¼ cup apple, diced

¼ cup carrot, diced

¼ cup leeks, sliced

1 garlic clove, minced

1 teaspoon flour

¼ cup apple cider vinegar

¾ cup chicken stock

1 teaspoon butter

Directions

Preheat the oven to 350°.

Place the olive oil in a small Dutch oven and cook over medium-high heat until it begins to sizzle. Season the chicken breast with salt and pepper, place it in the Dutch oven, and cook for 10 minutes. Turn the chicken breast over, cook for 5 more minutes, remove from the Dutch oven, and set aside.

Add the apple, carrot, leeks, and garlic to the Dutch oven and cook until soft. Add the flour and cook for 1 to 2 minutes. Add the apple cider vinegar to deglaze the Dutch oven.

Directions
(continued)

Add the chicken stock and cook until it boils. Return the chicken breast to the Dutch oven, cover it, and place in the oven. Cook for 40 to 50 minutes.

Remove the chicken breast from the Dutch oven and place on a plate. Add the butter to the Dutch oven, stir until combined, and then spoon the apple, carrots, and leeks over the chicken breast. Serve with rice or couscous.

MOROCCAN CHICKEN

This is essentially a one-pan meal that provides
way too much flavor for how easy it is.

ACTIVE TIME 30 MINUTES

Ingredients

1 10-ounce chicken breast

¼ cup white wine

1 tablespoon honey

1 teaspoon ground cumin

1 teaspoon ground coriander

¼ teaspoon chili powder

¼ teaspoon ground nutmeg

Salt and pepper to taste

½ onion, sliced

2 garlic cloves, minced

½ cup dried fruit (Golden raisins, prunes, apricots, and dates work well.)

Directions

Place all of the ingredients in a bowl and stir until combined. Place in the refrigerator and let sit for eight hours, or overnight.

Preheat oven to 400° and grease a small baking dish with olive oil. Take half of the fruit-and-spice mixture from the bowl and place on the bottom of the dish. Nestle the chicken breast into that mixture and then top it with the remaining fruit-and-spice mixture.

Place chicken into the oven and bake for 30 to 40 minutes, until it is cooked through. Remove from the oven, and serve over couscous.

One Pork Chop, Served Three Ways

A single pork chop can be purchased with the bone in, or the bone out—it can be cut thick, or cut very thin. And, if you choose the right chop for your recipe, you'll be sure to enjoy the versatility of this particular cut. Not only that, pork chops freeze extremely well, so you can easily stock up and have part of a delicious dinner ready to go on those nights you are cooking for yourself.

STUFFED PORK CHOP

This pork chop, stuffed with bread, parmesan,
and herbs, fills any dinner with flavorful joy.

ACTIVE TIME 30 MINUTES

Ingredients

1 6-ounce boneless pork chop

1 tablespoon olive oil

1 garlic clove, minced

1 piece of stale, crusty bread, diced

1 tablespoon parmesan cheese

2 tablespoons fresh herbs, chopped (Basil, parsley, chives, thyme, and oregano all work well.)

⅓ cup chicken broth

Salt and pepper to taste

Directions

Preheat oven to 375° and grease a small baking dish with olive oil.

Use a chef's knife to cut along one side of the pork chop and create a pocket for the stuffing. Slather the pork chop with olive oil, season generously with salt and pepper, and set aside.

Add the garlic, bread, parmesan, herbs, chicken broth, salt, and pepper to a bowl and stir until combined. Stuff the pork chop with this mixture and secure with toothpicks, if necessary. Place the pork chop into the oven and bake for 30 minutes, or until an instant-read thermometer reads 145° when inserted into the meat. Remove from the oven, and serve.

PAN-ROASTED PORK CHOP WITH SPICY TOMATO SALSA

The tomato salsa gives this recipe a nice kick.
It is also great with a grilled pork chop.

ACTIVE TIME 20 MINUTES

Ingredients

1 6-ounce pork chop

1 tablespoon olive oil

1 tablespoon butter

1 garlic clove, minced

2 green onions, chopped

½ cup fresh tomatoes, diced

½ jalapeño pepper

2 tablespoons cilantro, chopped

Salt and pepper to taste

Directions

Place the olive oil, butter, and garlic in a frying pan and cook over medium-high heat. While this is cooking, season the pork chop generously with salt and pepper.

When the garlic has begun to soften, place the pork chop in the pan and cook for 5 to 7 minutes on each side, until an instant-read thermometer reads 145° when inserted into the meat.

While the pork chop is cooking, add the tomatoes, jalapeño pepper, cilantro, salt, and pepper to a small bowl, stir until combined, and set aside.

When pork chop is finished cooking, place it on a plate, spoon the salsa over the top of it, and serve.

PAN-ROASTED PORK CHOP WITH APPLES, LEEKS, AND A CIDER GLAZE

This recipe, which works well with a bone-in chop, is a little more decadent than traditional pork chops and applesauce.

ACTIVE TIME 30 MINUTES

Ingredients

1 6-ounce pork chop

1 tablespoon olive oil

1 cup apple, diced

½ cup leeks, thinly sliced

1 garlic clove, minced

1 tablespoon butter

3 tablespoons apple cider vinegar

¼ cup apple cider

½ teaspoon Dijon mustard

4 to 5 fresh sage leaves

Salt and pepper to taste

Directions

Place the olive oil and butter in a frying pan and cook over medium-high heat until the butter is melted. Place the pork chop in the pan and cook for 5 to 7 minutes on each side, until an instant-read thermometer reads 145° when stuck into the meat. Remove from pan and set aside.

Add the apple, leeks, and garlic to the pan and cook until soft, approximately 5 minutes. Add the apple cider vinegar, apple cider, and Dijon mustard to the pan and cook until it bubbles. Add sage, salt, and pepper, and cook while stirring.

Directions
(continued)

When the sauce has thickened to desired consistency, place the pork chop on a plate, spoon the contents of the pan over it, and serve.

PORK SAUSAGE WITH CARAMELIZED ONIONS AND WILTED GREENS

This is a quick way to enjoy a hearty lunch or dinner, while still eating your greens. If you're looking for a larger meal, you can always add additional spinach.

ACTIVE TIME 20 MINUTES

Ingredients

2 medium-sized pork sausages

1 tablespoon olive oil

½ onion, thinly sliced

1 cup baby spinach

Directions

Place the olive oil in a frying pan and cook over medium-high heat until it begins to sizzle. Add the onion and cook until soft.

Add the sausages to the pan and cook, while turning, until they are browned and the onion has started to caramelize.

Turn the heat down to medium-low, add the spinach, stirring constantly until the spinach wilts, and then serve.

— CHAPTER FOUR —

Seafood

Seafood is often overlooked when cooking for one, but it can be the easiest way to treat yourself when cooking on your own. Typically, when purchasing fresh seafood, a pound of mussels or clams serves one, and 6 to 8 shrimp, depending on their size, are perfect. For fish, something between ¼ pound and ½ pound works well. Fish is also a great way to expand your repertoire as a cook, since the sauces and techniques seafood requires will serve you well elsewhere.

SCALLOPS WITH CHERRY TOMATOES AND BROWN BUTTER

Scallops are always a treat. And, when made with cherry tomatoes and brown butter, they become even more decadent.

ACTIVE TIME 20 MINUTES

Ingredients

¼ pound scallops (5 to 6 scallops)

1 tablespoon olive oil

1 tablespoon butter

2 tablespoons freshly squeezed lemon juice

½ cup cherry tomatoes

Directions

Place the oil in a frying pan and cook over medium-high heat. While the oil is heating up, season the scallops with salt and pepper.

When the oil begins to sizzle, place the scallops in the pan and cook for 3 minutes. Flip the scallops over and add the butter. Continue to cook, allowing butter to slowly brown.

Add the cherry tomatoes and cook for another 3 minutes, until tomatoes are cooked through and butter is a nutty brown color. Remove from heat and serve over rice or mashed potatoes, spooning the tomatoes and brown butter over the dish.

SHRIMP AND SUGAR SNAP PEA STIR-FRY

Shrimp stir-fry is easy to make—when prepped ahead it can be made in under 10 minutes! It's great on its own or served with rice.

ACTIVE TIME 20 MINUTES

Ingredients

6 to 8 medium-sized shrimp

1 tablespoon vegetable oil

1 garlic clove, minced

1 teaspoon ginger, minced

¼ teaspoon red chili flakes

Salt and pepper to taste

1 cup sugar snap peas

½ onion, thinly sliced

½ teaspoon sesame oil

Directions

Place the vegetable oil in a frying pan and cook over medium-high heat until the oil begins to sizzle. Add the garlic and ginger and cook until they are softened. Add the onion and cook, while constantly stirring and flipping the contents of the pan, until the onion begins to soften. Add the sugar snap peas and cook, while continuing to stir and flip the pan's contents.

Add the shrimp, red pepper flakes, salt, and pepper, and cook for an additional 3 minutes, or until shrimp turns pink.

Add the sesame oil to the pan and toss to coat. Serve over rice.

BAKED HADDOCK WITH BUTTER AND BREAD CRUMBS

A fresh filet of haddock with butter and bread crumbs can be baked with little effort. Served with a salad of mixed greens or some fresh, steamed vegetables, it's guaranteed to satisfy.

ACTIVE TIME 20 MINUTES

Ingredients

1 fresh filet of haddock, (approximately 6 to 8 ounces)

1 tablespoon butter

¼ cup fresh bread crumbs

⅛ teaspoon garlic powder

1 tablespoon fresh parsley, finely chopped

Salt and pepper to taste

1 wedge of lemon for garnish

Directions

Preheat oven to 400°. Place the bread crumbs, garlic powder, parsley, salt, and pepper in a bowl, stir to combine, and set aside.

Place 2 tablespoons of water in the bottom of a small baking dish. Place the filet in the dish, spoon the bread crumb mixture over it, and top with the butter. Place in the oven and bake for 10 to 12 minutes, or until the crumbs are golden brown.

Remove dish from the oven, garnish with the lemon wedge, and serve with a mixed green salad or a vegetable.

Mussels, with Three Broths

Mussels can be enjoyed throughout the year with a
variety of delicious broths and sauces. They go perfectly
with crusty bread and a mixed green salad.

MUSSELS WITH COCONUT CURRY BROTH

ACTIVE TIME 20 MINUTES

Ingredients

1 pound of fresh mussels, scrubbed and cleaned

1 tablespoon olive oil

1 garlic clove, minced

3 shallots, minced

1 teaspoon fresh ginger, minced

½ jalapeño pepper, minced

1 teaspoon red curry paste

¼ cup white wine

½ cup coconut milk

Salt to taste

¼ cup basil leaves, chopped, for garnish

1 tablespoon freshly squeezed lime juice for garnish

Lime wedges for garnish

Directions

Place the olive oil, garlic, shallots, and ginger in a Dutch oven and cook over medium-high heat until the garlic begins to soften. Add the jalapeño pepper and the curry paste, and cook while stirring. After 2 to 3 minutes, add the wine and coconut milk and bring to a boil. Add the salt and the mussels, cover the Dutch oven, and cook for 5 minutes.

Remove the cover from the Dutch oven and discard any unopened mussels. Transfer contents of Dutch oven to a bowl, garnish with basil, lime juice, and lime wedges, and serve.

MUSSELS WITH SPICY MARINARA SAUCE

This one will transport you to the coast of Italy. Because of this, it's perfect with crusty bread, or over pasta.

ACTIVE TIME 20 MINUTES

Ingredients

1 pound of fresh mussels, scrubbed and cleaned

1 tablespoon olive oil

¼ onion, diced

¼ cup red wine

½ cup canned diced tomatoes, with juice

¼ cup tomato sauce [See recipe on page 125.]

¼ teaspoon red pepper flakes

Salt and pepper to taste

¼ cup basil leaves, chopped, for garnish

Directions

Place the olive oil and onion in a small Dutch oven and cook over medium-high heat until the onion begins to soften. Add the wine, tomatoes, and tomato sauce, and bring to a gentle boil.

Add the red pepper flakes, salt, and pepper. Add the mussels, cover the Dutch oven, and cook for 5 minutes.

Remove the cover, discard any unopened mussels, and transfer contents of Dutch oven to a bowl. Garnish with the basil and serve.

MUSSELS WITH GARLIC, BUTTER, AND WHITE WINE

This one is a classic for a reason. Enjoy with a glass
of white wine, and you'll understand why.

ACTIVE TIME 20 MINUTES

Ingredients

1 pound of fresh mussels,
scrubbed and cleaned

1 tablespoon olive oil

2 tablespoons butter

2 shallots, minced

1 garlic clove, minced

½ cup white wine

Fresh lemon wedges
for garnish

Directions

Place the olive oil, butter, shallots, and garlic in a Dutch oven
and cook over medium-high heat until the garlic and shallots
begin to soften. Add the wine and bring to a low boil. Add salt
and pepper, and then add the mussels. Cover the Dutch oven and
cook for 5 minutes.

Remove cover and discard any unopened mussels. Transfer
contents of Dutch oven to a bowl, garnish with fresh lemon
wedges, and serve.

— CHAPTER FIVE —

Bowls

"The Bowl" is an obvious choice for a one-person meal, and it's all the rage at the moment. As long as you keep your fridge and pantry well-stocked, you'll be able to enjoy the benefits of this culinary revolution. The nice thing about the bowl is that it is intended for one, and can easily be doled out across the evening, making it ideal for the busy family that eats at different times.

The bowl is good-looking, nourishing, delicious, and easy to alter. And if that isn't enough to sell you, it's also a snap to clean up, since there's just a bowl and a utensil. So stock that kitchen and clean those bowls—a new day has dawned!

GRILLED FLANK STEAK AND SWEET POTATO BOWL

As the steak and sweet potatoes in this bowl are grilled, it's perfect for a summer evening, when you want to keep your cooking outdoors.

ACTIVE TIME 20 MINUTES

Ingredients

3 oz. piece of flank steak

1 sweet potato

2 tablespoons olive oil

2 tablespoons apple cider vinegar

Salt and pepper to taste

½ cup brown rice, cooked

½ cup black beans, drained and rinsed

½ avocado, sliced

2 tablespoons fresh cilantro, chopped

2 tablespoons salsa verde

Honey-Lime Dressing:

2 teaspoons olive oil

1 teaspoon honey

2 teaspoons freshly squeezed lime juice

2 teaspoons adobo sauce

Directions

Approximately 1 hour before you begin to cook, combine the olive oil, apple cider vinegar, salt, and pepper in a small bowl. Add the piece of flank steak and let it marinate until you are ready to grill.

Poke holes in the sweet potato, place it in the microwave, and microwave on high until soft, approximately 8 to 10 minutes. Remove the sweet potato and cut the flesh into cubes.

Preheat your gas or charcoal grill. When it is ready, place the flank steak and the cubed sweet potato on the grill. For medium rare, cook the steak for 5 minutes on each side. Cook the sweet potato until a fork can easily be inserted.

Directions
(continued)

Prepare the dressing: Add the olive oil, honey, lime juice, and adobo sauce to a small bowl, whisk until combined, and set aside.

Add the brown rice and salsa verde to a bowl and toss. When combined, top with the grilled flank steak, sweet potato cubes, black beans, avocado, and chopped cilantro. Drizzle the dressing over the bowl, and serve.

GRILLED SHRIMP AND MANGO BOWL

This bowl uses the clean flavor of shrimp and the sweetness of mango to transport you to the tropics. Grilled scallops or fish can be substituted for the shrimp.

ACTIVE TIME 20 MINUTES

Ingredients

8 medium shrimp, shelled and deveined

½ cup fresh mango, diced

½ cup green cabbage, chopped

½ cup brown rice, cooked

1 tablespoon cilantro, chopped

¼ cup shredded, unsweetened coconut

¼ cup salted peanuts

Cilantro-Lime Dressing:

2 tablespoons olive oil

1 garlic clove, minced

1 tablespoon cilantro, chopped

2 tablespoons fresh lime juice

Directions

Prepare the dressing: Add the olive oil, garlic, cilantro, and lime juice to a bowl, whisk until combined, and set aside.

Preheat your gas or charcoal grill. When it is ready, place the shrimp on the grill and cook for 3 to 4 minutes on each side. When the shrimp is cooked through, remove from the grill and let them cool slightly.

Add the brown rice and cilantro to a bowl and toss until combined. Top with the grilled shrimp, cabbage, mango, shredded coconut, and peanuts. Drizzle with the dressing and serve.

SUMMER CORN AND TOMATO BOWL

Combining two seasonal favorites, corn and tomatoes, in one bowl makes for a great summer lunch or dinner.

ACTIVE TIME 15 MINUTES

Ingredients

Kernels from 2 ears of steamed sweet corn

1 tomato, cubed

½ cup of mixed greens

1 cup white rice, cooked

¼ cup of alfalfa sprouts

¼ cup blanched, chopped asparagus

Squeeze of fresh lemon

Buttermilk Dressing with Parmesan:

1 garlic clove, minced

Black pepper to taste

½ teaspoon apple cider vinegar

½ teaspoon Worcestershire sauce

⅛ cup buttermilk

⅛ cup mayonnaise

¼ cup freshly grated parmesan cheese

Directions

Prepare the dressing: Add the garlic, black pepper, apple cider vinegar, Worcestershire sauce, buttermilk, mayonnaise, and parmesan cheese to a bowl, whisk until combined, and set aside.

Add the rice to a bowl and squeeze the lemon over it. Top with mixed greens, corn, tomatoes, alfalfa sprouts, and asparagus. Drizzle the dressing over the bowl, and serve.

BLT BOWL

It's a deconstructed classic bacon, lettuce, and tomato sandwich, with a lovely, simple buttermilk dressing to replace the mayonnaise.

ACTIVE TIME 20 MINUTES

Ingredients

3 slices of thick-cut bacon

1 cup mixed greens

1 cup tomato, diced

1 cup white rice, cooked

Squeeze of fresh lemon juice

¼ cup homemade croutons

Buttermilk Dressing:

1 garlic clove, minced

Black pepper to taste

½ teaspoon apple cider vinegar

½ teaspoon Worcestershire sauce

⅛ cup buttermilk

⅛ cup mayonnaise

Directions

Place the bacon in a frying pan and cook over medium heat until it is crispy. Remove from pan, allow to drain on a paper towel, and slice into bite-sized pieces.

Buttermilk Dressing:

Add the garlic, black pepper, apple cider vinegar, Worcestershire sauce, buttermilk, and mayonnaise to a bowl, whisk until combined, and set aside.

Place the rice in a bowl and squeeze the lemon over it. Top with mixed greens, tomatoes, and bacon, drizzle the dressing over the bowl, and serve.

To make your own croutons preheat oven to 350°. Toss a cup of cubed, day old bread, roll, or baguette with 1 tablespoon olive oil, ½ teaspoon garlic salt, and black pepper to taste. Spread out on cookie sheet and bake until golden brown.

SPICY WHITE BEAN BURRITO BOWL

Essentially a bean burrito, just without the tortilla.
If you're a fan of spice, don't hold back here—the
beans can be prepared as spicy as you like.

ACTIVE TIME 15 MINUTES

Ingredients

15 oz. can of white beans

⅛ teaspoon ground cumin

1 garlic clove, minced

⅛ teaspoon jalapeño pepper, minced

1⅓ tablespoons cilantro, chopped

½ cup brown rice, cooked

¼ cup mixed greens

½ cup cucumber, diced

¼ cup salsa

¼ cup queso fresco

Squeeze of fresh lime juice

Directions

Add white beans, cumin, garlic, jalapeño, and 1 tablespoon of the cilantro to a small saucepan and cook over medium heat for 10 minutes, or until the beans start to bubble.

Remove the saucepan from the heat and pour the beans into a bowl. Top with the brown rice, the squeeze of lime juice, and the remaining cilantro. Add the mixed greens, cucumber, and salsa, top with the queso fresco, and serve.

SPINACH, QUINOA, AND CHICKEN BOWL

This hearty bowl benefits a good deal from the addition of pesto. Trust me, this one's guaranteed to satisfy.

ACTIVE TIME 20 MINUTES

Ingredients

1 medium boneless, skinless chicken breast

1 cup quinoa, cooked

½ cup cherry tomatoes

½ cup brussels sprouts, steamed

½ avocado, sliced

½ cup cucumbers, sliced

2 tablespoons pesto

2 cups baby spinach

2 tablespoons toasted sesame seeds for garnish

Directions

Preheat your gas or charcoal grill. When it is ready, place the chicken breast on the grill and cook for 5 minutes on each side. When it is cooked through, remove from grill and allow to cool slightly. When it is cool enough to handle, cut into bite-sized cubes and set aside.

Add the pesto to the saucepan containing the recently cooked quinoa and stir to combine. Add the baby spinach and stir until it wilts.

Add the contents of the saucepan to a bowl. Top with grilled chicken, cherry tomatoes, brussels sprouts, avocado, and cucumbers, garnish with the sesame seeds, and serve.

GRILLED CHICKEN BOWL WITH GRILLED ASPARAGUS AND AVOCADO

Throw the chicken, asparagus, and avocado on the grill and toss this bowl together in a matter of minutes.

ACTIVE TIME 20 MINUTES

Ingredients

1 chicken breast, grilled and sliced

1 cup rice, cooked

1 tablespoon lime juice

1 tablespoon cilantro, chopped

1 lime, quartered

½ avocado, sliced and grilled

8 spears of asparagus, grilled

Salt and pepper to taste

Directions

Combine the rice, lime juice, cilantro, salt, and pepper in a bowl.

Top with the chicken, avocado, and asparagus, garnish with the lime quarters, and serve.

CLASSIC TUNA POKE BOWL

This classic, made with raw tuna, just may have started the bowl craze. Check it out, and you'll see what got everyone so excited.

ACTIVE TIME 20 MINUTES

Ingredients

¼ pound sushi grade ahi tuna, cubed

½ avocado, sliced

¼ cup radishes, sliced

¼ cucumber, sliced

1 cup white rice, cooked

1 teaspoon sesame oil

⅛ teaspoon red pepper flakes

1 teaspoon rice wine vinegar

1 teaspoon toasted sesame seeds for garnish

⅛ cup green onions, sliced, for garnish

Directions

Add the sesame oil, red pepper flakes, and rice wine vinegar to a bowl and stir to combine. Place the tuna into the bowl and let it marinate for at least 30 minutes.

Place the rice in a bowl. Top with the tuna, avocado, radishes, and cucumbers, garnish with the toasted sesame seeds and green onions, and serve.

SALMON TERIYAKI BOWL

Healthy, delicious food doesn't get any simpler than fresh, seared salmon and a simple homemade teriyaki sauce served over soba noodles. If you like your sweet with a little heat, be sure to use the chili pepper.

ACTIVE TIME 20 MINUTES

Ingredients

1 bunch soba noodles

1 salmon filet, approximately 5 ounces

1 tablespoon canola oil

½ cup teriyaki sauce [See recipe that follows.]

Salt and pepper to taste

1 red chili pepper, optional

Sesame seeds for garnish

Cilantro for garnish

Teriyaki Sauce:

1 cup soy sauce

½ cup dark brown sugar

1 cup mirin (Japanese cooking wine)

½ cup sake

Directions

Bring a small pot of water to boil. Salt to taste, add soba noodles, and cook according to manufacturer's instructions. Once cooked, drain and place in bowl.

As the noodles are cooking, pat the salmon filet dry with paper towels and then season with salt and pepper.

Place the oil in a skillet and cook over medium-high heat until the oil shimmers.

Add chili pepper, if using, and sear until cooked on all sides. Remove and set aside.

Add the salmon, skin-side down, to the skillet, and reduce heat to medium-low. Cook until skin is crisp, approximately 6 minutes.

Flip salmon and cook for approximately 3 more minutes for medium-rare, 4 minutes for medium. Remove salmon from the skillet and set on a paper towel-lined plate to drain.

Directions
(continued)

Brush filet with teriyaki sauce to taste. If using, chop cooked chili pepper.

Place salmon on bed of soba noodles and add chopped chili pepper, if using. Garnish with sesame seeds and cilantro and serve.

Teriyaki Sauce:

Combine all ingredients in small saucepan. Bring mixture to a boil and then reduce heat so that it simmers. Cook until mixture is reduced enough to coat back of a spoon, approximately 20 minutes. Remove from heat and use immediately.

CHAPTER SIX

Pasta

Pasta is often the dinner you think about when you're going to cook for yourself. The old cliché of cooking some spaghetti and cracking open a jar of prepared sauce for a quick, comforting meal exists for a reason.

These pasta recipes are a step-up, using fresh ingredients and keeping an eye toward making the meal special. Many of these recipes are almost as easy as cooking the pasta and cracking open a jar, only with more delicious results. Trust me, having fresh herbs and a block of parmesan cheese around will always take your pasta game to another level.

TIPS:

* Boxed pasta can be divided easily into single-serving portions. For spaghetti or linguine, a one-pound box can be divided into three to four portions, each one secured with a sandwich tie or kitchen string. Store these bundles until you're ready to grab one. Loose pasta can be measured out and stored in individual bags or small glass jars for the same easy-to-use, one-portion size. And sheets of no-boil lasagna can be broken into thirds to create the perfectly sized components of a one-serving lasagna.

* When cooking pasta, make sure to generously salt the water before adding the pasta.

* As a few recipes in this chapter call for tomato sauce, the following is a simple, delicious recipe that you can whip up in no time; and, when cooking for one, the beauty of this sauce is that it freezes beautifully.

TOMATO SAUCE FOR ONE

Ingredients

1 tablespoon olive oil

2 garlic cloves, minced

1 cup canned tomatoes,
or 2 to 3 plum tomatoes,
peeled and chopped

1 tablespoon tomato paste

¼ cup broth

Splash of red wine

½ teaspoon oregano

½ teaspoon basil

Salt and pepper to taste

Directions

Place the olive oil and the garlic in a small saucepan and cook over medium heat until the garlic has softened. Add the tomatoes and continue to cook, while stirring frequently. Add the broth, red wine, oregano, basil, salt, and pepper, and simmer for 20 minutes.

WINTER OR SUMMER CHERRY TOMATO AND OLIVE PASTA

Colorful on the plate or in the bowl, this pasta packs plenty of flavor. The cherry tomatoes can be prepared two different ways, depending on the season.

ACTIVE TIME SUMMER VERSION, 25 MINUTES; WINTER VERSION, 50 MINUTES

Ingredients

1½ cups of your favorite pasta

1 tablespoon olive oil

1 garlic clove, minced

1 cup of cherry tomatoes, halved

1 handful of your favorite olives, pitted and chopped

Salt and pepper to taste

Freshly grated parmesan for garnish

Directions

Summer Version:

Bring water to boil in a medium saucepan. When water is boiling, add pasta and cook until al dente.

While pasta is cooking, cut tomatoes and chop olives.

Add the olive oil and the garlic to a frying pan and cook over medium heat until the oil begins to sizzle and the garlic starts to soften.

Add tomatoes and olives to the pan and stir. Cook until the tomatoes and olives are cooked through.

When pasta is ready, drain and return to the saucepan. Add the contents of the frying pan and toss until combined.

Garnish with parmesan cheese and serve.

Winter Version:
Preheat oven to 400°.

Directions
(continued)

Add olive oil, garlic, tomatoes, and olives to a bowl and toss until the oil evenly coats everything. Spread them on a parchment-lined baking sheet, place in oven, and roast for 30 minutes.

When the vegetables have been roasting for approximately 10 minutes, bring water to boil in a medium saucepan. When the water is boiling, add pasta and cook until al dente.

Remove baking sheet from the oven. Drain pasta, return to the saucepan, and toss with the roasted garlic, tomatoes, and olives, adding additional olive oil if necessary.

Garnish with the parmesan cheese and serve.

PANCETTA, LEMON, CHILI, AND BRIGHT GREENS WITH ANGEL HAIR PASTA

Spicy chili flakes and salty pancetta, when combined with tart lemon and bright baby spinach, make this a pasta dish worthy of a celebration. It can more than stand on its own, but a glass of Beaujolais is a great addition.

ACTIVE TIME 20 MINUTES

Ingredients

1½ cups of angel hair pasta

1 tablespoon olive oil

2 garlic cloves, minced

3 to 4 slices of pancetta, cut into slivers

½ teaspoon chili flakes

¼ cup freshly squeezed lemon juice

1 tablespoon lemon zest

1 cup of baby spinach

Salt and pepper to taste

Freshly grated parmesan cheese for garnish

Directions

Bring water to boil in a medium saucepan. When water is boiling, add pasta and cook until al dente.

While pasta is cooking, add olive oil and garlic to a frying pan and cook over medium heat until the garlic begins to soften.

Add the slivers of pancetta and chili flakes to the pan and continue to cook until the meat begins to sizzle and brown around the edges.

When the pasta has finished cooking, drain and add to the frying pan. Use tongs to toss until combined.

Add lemon juice, lemon zest, and baby spinach to the pan and continue to toss until the greens begin to wilt.

Add salt and pepper to taste, garnish with parmesan cheese, and serve.

LINGUINE WITH RICOTTA, ARUGULA, AND LEMON

This pasta is fast, flavorful, and can be prepared with a variety of pastas. If arugula is out of reach, it can also be made with baby spinach or dandelion greens.

ACTIVE TIME 20 MINUTES

Ingredients

1 ½ cups linguine, cooked

1 cup fresh arugula

¼ cup freshly squeezed lemon juice

1 tablespoon lemon zest

½ cup ricotta cheese

1 tablespoon butter, softened

Salt and pepper to taste

Freshly grated parmesan cheese for garnish

Directions

Bring water to boil in a medium saucepan. When water is boiling, add pasta and cook until al dente. When the pasta is ready, drain while reserving ¼ cup of the water.

Add the lemon juice, lemon zest, ricotta cheese, butter, and hot pasta water to a small bowl and stir until creamy.

Return pasta to the saucepan, add the ricotta mixture, and toss.

Fold in arugula and toss until the greens wilt slightly.

Add salt and pepper to taste, garnish with parmesan cheese, and serve.

PASTA WITH TOASTED GARLIC CRUMBS AND PARMESAN

Many Italians consider this dish a favorite comfort food, put together with ingredients that are always on hand. Made for one, it is best enjoyed with a green salad and a glass of Chianti.

ACTIVE TIME 20 MINUTES

Ingredients

1½ cups of your favorite pasta

2 tablespoons olive oil

2 garlic cloves, minced

1 cup fresh bread crumbs

Salt and pepper to taste

Freshly grated parmesan cheese for garnish

Directions

Bring water to boil in a medium saucepan. When water is boiling, add pasta and cook until al dente.

While the pasta is cooking, cook the olive oil and garlic in a frying pan over medium heat until the oil begins to sizzle and the garlic starts to soften.

Add the fresh bread crumbs to the frying pan and stir until they begin to toast and are coated with the olive oil and garlic.

When the pasta is finished cooking, drain and then add it to the frying pan. Stir until the pasta is coated by the bread crumbs, olive oil, and garlic.

Add salt and pepper to taste, garnish with plenty of parmesan cheese, and serve.

ASPARAGUS CARBONARA

Asparagus is available all year in most places, but when it's in season in your area, you should definitely grab it. This dish focuses on the simple flavor of the asparagus— so if you really love it, feel free to add an entire bundle.

ACTIVE TIME 30 MINUTES

Ingredients

1 ½ cups penne pasta

½ bundle of asparagus, woody ends chopped off, cut into bite-sized pieces

¼ cup pancetta, cubed

½ cup baby peas

2 tablespoons toasted pine nuts

1 tablespoon butter

2 eggs

¼ cup heavy cream

¼ cup of freshly grated parmesan cheese, plus more for garnish

Salt and pepper to taste

Directions

Bring water to boil in a medium saucepan. When water is boiling, add pasta and cook until al dente.

While the pasta is cooking, bring water to boil in a small saucepan and then add the asparagus. Cook for 1 minute, blanch, and set aside.

Add the pancetta and butter to a frying pan and cook over medium heat until the pancetta is cooked through. Add the blanched asparagus and the peas.

Directions
(continued)

Add the eggs, heavy cream, parmesan cheese, salt, and pepper to a small bowl and stir until combined.

When the pasta is finished cooking, drain and then add to the frying pan. Toss briefly, add the egg, cream, and parmesan mixture to the pan, and toss until the pasta is coated and the eggs are cooked.

Garnish with additional grated parmesan cheese and serve.

GARLIC AND CLAM LINGUINE

This dish is best made with fresh clams. When
selecting clams at a seafood counter, a dozen with
shells is a good amount for a single serving.

ACTIVE TIME 30 MINUTES

Ingredients

¼ pound linguine

12 fresh clams, freshly scrubbed
and soaked in cold water

2 garlic cloves, minced

1 tablespoon olive oil

¼ cup white wine

1 teaspoon anchovy paste

⅛ teaspoon red chili flakes

2 tablespoons freshly chopped
parsley for garnish

Freshly grated parmesan
cheese for garnish

Directions

Bring water to boil in a medium saucepan. When water is
boiling, add pasta and cook until al dente.

While the linguine is cooking, cook the garlic, olive oil,
anchovy paste, and red chili flakes in a frying pan over
medium heat until the garlic is soft.

Add white wine and continue to cook. Add the clams directly
to the frying pan and cover. The clams will start to open as
they cook. Cook for 5 minutes, and discard any clams with
unopened shells.

Drain the pasta, making sure to reserve some of the cooking water. Add the pasta to the frying pan. If it looks like the clams may need more liquid, add the pasta water a little at a time. Use tongs to toss the contents of the frying pan until they are well-combined.

Pour the contents of the pan into a bowl, guiding the clams, which should still be in their shells, to the top of the bowl. Garnish with the parsley and parmesan cheese, and serve.

SUMMER ZUCCHINI PASTA WITH CREAM AND PEPPER

When zucchini season arrives, this pasta goes into regular rotation.
It works really well with rotini or penne, but any pasta will do.

ACTIVE TIME 25 MINUTES

Ingredients

1 ½ cups pasta, preferably rotini or penne

1 tablespoon butter

1 garlic clove, minced

1 tablespoon flour

¼ cup half-and-half

¼ cup freshly grated parmesan cheese

½ zucchini, shredded

Salt and pepper to taste

¼ cup cherry tomatoes

Directions

Bring water to boil in a medium saucepan. When water is boiling, add pasta and cook until al dente.

While pasta is cooking, add the butter and garlic to a saucepan and cook over medium heat until the garlic has softened. Add the flour and cook for a couple of minutes, stirring frequently. Add half-and-half and continue to stir. Add the zucchini and cook until the sauce begins to bubble.

When the pasta has finished cooking, drain it and then add it to the saucepan containing the zucchini. Stir until well-combined.

Add parmesan cheese, salt, pepper, and cherry tomatoes, and serve.

SPINACH AND MUSHROOM LASAGNA

This lasagna is a great vegetarian option. Use a variety of mushrooms to add a greater depth of flavor to this recipe.

ACTIVE TIME 1 HOUR

Ingredients

1 sheet of cooked lasagna or one sheet of no-boil lasagna, split into three pieces

1 cup spinach

1 cup mushrooms, chopped (Portobello, oyster, white, and cremini all work well and are readily available.)

¼ cup vegetable broth

1 tablespoon olive oil

1 garlic clove, minced

½ teaspoon oregano

½ teaspoon basil

¼ cup ricotta cheese

2 tablespoons parmesan cheese, grated

3 tablespoons fresh mozzarella, shredded

Salt and pepper to taste

Directions

Preheat oven to 350°.

Add the olive oil and garlic to a frying pan and cook over medium heat until the garlic has softened. Add mushrooms, broth, oregano, basil, salt, and pepper to the pan, and cook until the mushrooms soften. Add the spinach and cook until it begins to wilt. Remove the pan from heat and set aside.

Add the ricotta, parmesan cheese, salt, and pepper to a small bowl, stir to combine, and set aside.

Cover the bottom of a very small baking dish with approximately ¼ cup of the mixture in the frying pan. Top with a piece of lasagna noodle, add the ricotta mixture, and then place another piece of lasagna noodle on top. Add another layer of the mixture from the pan, add the last piece of noodle, and then top with the mozzarella.

Place the baking dish in the oven and bake for 25 minutes. The mozzarella should be golden brown when the lasagna is ready. Remove from the oven and serve.

SOLO LASAGNA

Lasagna is usually served in a large pan for a big crowd, but it's easy to make for one person, filled with cheese and a delicious meat sauce. There is extra sauce in this recipe, in case you want to spoon it over the top.

ACTIVE TIME 1 HOUR

Ingredients

1 sheet of fresh lasagna or one sheet of no-boil lasagna, split into three pieces

1 cup tomato sauce [See recipe on page 125.]

¼ pound ground beef

1 tablespoon olive oil

1 garlic clove, minced

½ teaspoon oregano

½ teaspoon basil

¼ cup ricotta cheese

2 tablespoons parmesan cheese, grated

3 tablespoons fresh mozzarella, shredded

Salt and pepper to taste

Directions

Preheat oven to 350°.

Add the olive oil, garlic, and ground beef to a frying pan and cook over medium heat until the beef is cooked through. Add the tomato sauce, oregano, basil, salt, and pepper, and cook until the sauce begins to bubble, approximately 10 minutes. Set pan aside.

Add the ricotta, parmesan cheese, salt, and pepper to a small bowl and combine. Set the bowl aside.

Cover the bottom of a very small baking dish with approximately ¼ cup of the meat sauce. Top with a piece of lasagna noodle, add a layer of the ricotta mixture, and top with another piece of the lasagna noodle. Add another layer of meat sauce, add the last piece of noodle, and top with the mozzarella.

Place dish in the oven and bake for 25 minutes. The mozzarella should be golden brown when the lasagna is ready.

Remove the dish from the oven and serve, topping the lasagna with any remaining sauce.

SPAGHETTI AND
A MEATBALL

Spaghetti dinners conjure up images of a crowd. But that doesn't mean there's still not something special about sitting down to a plate of spaghetti with just one meatball.

ACTIVE TIME 45 MINUTES

Ingredients

1 ½ cups spaghetti

1 tablespoon olive oil

1 garlic clove, minced

1 shallot, minced

1 cup tomato sauce
[See recipe on page 125.]

½ teaspoon basil

½ teaspoon oregano

⅛ pound ground beef

2 tablespoons Italian bread crumbs

1 tablespoon mayonnaise

Salt and pepper to taste

Directions

Bring water to boil in a medium saucepan. When water is boiling, add pasta and cook until al dente.

Add olive oil, garlic, and the shallot to a saucepan and cook over medium heat until the garlic and shallot are soft. Add the tomato sauce, herbs, salt, and pepper, and cook for 15 minutes, until the sauce is bubbling.

Add the ground beef, Italian bread crumbs, mayonnaise, salt, and pepper to a small bowl, combine, and form into one large meatball.

Directions
(continued)

Heat olive oil in a small frying pan over medium heat. Add meatball to the pan and cook until completely browned. Remove and add to the sauce.

Drain the pasta and place on a plate. When the meatball is cooked through, top the pasta with the sauce and the meatball, and serve.

CHAPTER SEVEN

Vegetables

Many of the recipes in this chapter make stand-alone lunches or dinners, but they can also accompany meat, chicken, or fish. And for vegetables that can practically get sliced in half, like acorn squash and zucchini, there is an opportunity for a couple of meals. When it comes to vegetables, the fresher the better. Even if you don't have a garden, shopping seasonally and locally makes a big difference in quality and flavor. Many large grocery store chains feature local produce sections. Local CSA's offer great produce, but they typically come in large quantities. This might be a good opportunity to split up a CSA box with friends or neighbors, to ensure there isn't waste.

CHERRY TOMATO CONFIT

In the heat of tomato season, tomato confit is the perfect way to use up the bountiful harvest. If you don't have a garden, don't worry—pints of lovely cherry tomatoes can always be found at the farmers market or at the grocery store. This can be served in a bowl of pasta or spooned over grilled fish or chicken. It's also great on top of a salad.

ACTIVE TIME 30 MINUTES **MAKES** APPROXIMATELY 4 CUPS

Ingredients

2 pints cherry tomatoes

6 garlic cloves

5 sprigs thyme

1 sprig rosemary

6 sage leaves

1 teaspoon kosher salt

2 cups olive oil

Directions

Preheat oven to 350°.

Place the tomatoes, garlic, thyme, rosemary, sage, kosher salt, and olive oil in a loaf pan. The oil should cover everything. Wrap a loaf pan tightly with aluminum foil and bake for 45 minutes to an hour, until the tomatoes and garlic are soft.

Remove the pan from the oven and allow the confit to cool. When it has cooled, place in a large glass jar with a top and transfer to the refrigerator, where it will last for two weeks.

ACORN SQUASH WITH APPLE AND QUINOA STUFFING

This dish is delicious in the fall, when the apples and squash are harvested. But it can be enjoyed year-round. Two halves of squash are good for two meals, so you can use one for lunch the next day, or with a salad tomorrow night.

ACTIVE TIME 30 MINUTES

Ingredients

1 acorn squash, halved and seeded

2 tablespoons olive oil

2 garlic cloves, minced

1 small apple, peeled and diced

1 ½ tablespoons chopped fresh herbs (Rosemary, sage, and thyme are good choices.)

2 cups quinoa, cooked

Salt and pepper to taste

Directions

Preheat oven to 350° and line a baking dish with aluminum foil or parchment paper. Place the squash face up on the baking dish and set aside.

Heat the olive oil in a saucepan over medium heat and then add the garlic. Cook until the garlic has softened, add the apples and herbs, and cook until the apples have softened. Add the quinoa and stir until it is moist.

Add salt and pepper to the saucepan and then remove it from the heat. Fill each half of acorn squash with the stuffing. Fill the baking dish with a ½-inch of water, cover the dish tightly with aluminum foil, place in oven, and bake for 1 hour.

QUINOA AND VEGETABLE SALAD WITH LEMON HERB DRESSING

Combining quinoa, fresh vegetables, and lemons has the capacity to make anything this dish accompanies feel special.

ACTIVE TIME 30 MINUTES

Ingredients

Dressing:

3 tablespoons olive oil

2 garlic cloves, minced

2 tablespoons fresh herbs, finely chopped (Chives, cilantro, basil, thyme, and parsley all work well.)

½ cup freshly squeezed lemon juice

Salt and pepper to taste

Salad:

1½ cups quinoa, cooked

½ cup cucumbers, chopped

½ tomato, diced

½ cup baby arugula

Salt and pepper to taste

Directions

Place the ingredients for the dressing into a glass jar with a top. Shake well and set aside.

Combine quinoa, cucumbers, tomato, and dressing in a bowl, and toss until the dressing is evenly distributed. Add salt and pepper and serve on a bed of the arugula.

VEGETABLE ROAST WITH CUMIN AND TAHINI DRESSING

This dish can be served hot or at room temperature. It's also versatile—you can substitute whatever you may have on hand for any of the vegetables.

ACTIVE TIME 40 MINUTES

Ingredients

Roasted Vegetables:

2 tablespoons olive oil

Salt and pepper to taste

½ cup carrots, peeled and sliced into rounds

1 garlic bulb, halved

½ cup beets, quartered

½ cup onion, cut into rings

½ cup butternut squash, cut into chunks

½ cup eggplant, cut into chunks

Chopped fresh parsley for garnish

Tahini Dressing:

⅓ cup tahini

3 tablespoons lemon juice

2 tablespoons honey

2 garlic cloves, minced

½ teaspoon cumin

½ teaspoon sea salt

Water to thin dressing, if necessary

Directions

Preheat oven to 375° and line a baking sheet with parchment paper.

Place prepared vegetables, olive oil, salt, and pepper in a large plastic bag and toss until the vegetables are evenly coated. Spread the vegetables onto a baking sheet and place it in the oven. Cook for 30 to 40 minutes, removing the sheet halfway through to flip the vegetables over.

Remove from oven and place on a plate. Drizzle with tahini dressing, garnish with parsley, and serve.

Tahini Dressing:

Place the tahini, lemon juice, honey, garlic, cumin, and sea salt in a food processor and blend until smooth. Add water to thin dressing, if necessary.

GREEN GODDESS DRESSING SERVED WITH BLANCHED GREEN AND YELLOW BEANS

The brightness on the plate makes this dish worth the effort.
It can easily accompany a meal, and it's lovely on its own,
enjoyed on a sunny afternoon with a glass of rosé.

ACTIVE TIME 20 MINUTES **MAKES** 2 SERVINGS

Ingredients

½ cup plain Greek yogurt

¼ cup mayonnaise

¼ cup lemon juice

2 green onions, with 3 inches
of green stem left on

2 garlic cloves

½ cup fresh parsley

¼ cup fresh cilantro

¼ cup fresh basil

2 cups yellow and green beans,
trimmed

Directions

Fill a large saucepan with water and bring to a boil. When the
water is boiling, add the green and yellow beans and cook for
approximately 2 to 3 minutes. Drain pot and drop the beans into
an ice bath to blanch them. Drain and arrange beans on a plate,
leaving a bit of room in the center of the plate.

Place all of the remaining ingredients in a blender or food
processor, and blend until smooth. Pour dressing into a small dish,
place it in the center of the plate filled with beans, and serve.

TOMATO WITH ANCHOVY AND HERB STUFFING

In the height of tomato season, when heirlooms are at their peak, this recipe will be bursting with flavor.

ACTIVE TIME 20 MINUTES

Ingredients

1 large tomato

1 tablespoon olive oil

2 anchovy filets, diced

2 tablespoons fresh herbs, chopped (Chives, basil, cilantro, and parsley work well.)

2 tablespoons freshly squeezed lemon juice

¾ cup orzo, cooked

½ cup arugula

Directions

Scoop the center out of the tomato and set the tomato aside. Remove the seeds from the flesh you have taken from the center and add this, the olive oil, anchovy filets, herbs, and lemon to a blender or food processor. Pulse until smooth.

In a small bowl, add the tomato mixture to the cooked orzo and toss until well-combined.

Fill the tomato with the orzo-and-tomato mixture. Top with bread crumbs. Serve over arugula with a fresh squeeze of lemon.

— CHAPTER EIGHT —

Make-Ahead Meals

Using one main element and creating numerous meals from that can change your whole week, making preparation a pleasure, and guaranteeing that you're in the right frame of mind to enjoy your meal when you sit down. This is the perfect way to cook for one, allowing you to stretch things that would typically be reserved for an entire family—such as a roast chicken or a pork loin—across an entire week of deliciousness. The lesson in this chapter is this: Just because you're one person, don't be afraid to think big on occasion— it just may make your entire week.

One Roast Chicken—Five meals

ROAST CHICKEN

The gift that keeps on giving. Not only will it start your week off right, it'll guarantee you eat well for the remainder of it.

ACTIVE TIME 20 MINUTES

Ingredients

1 whole chicken, 4 to 5 pounds

1 lemon, quartered

1 cup new baby potatoes

2 tablespoons olive oil

Salt and pepper to taste

Directions

Preheat your oven to 400°. While it is heating, use a paper or cotton towel to pat the chicken dry. Grease a roasting pan with cooking spray or olive oil, place the chicken in the pan, and rub it with the olive oil. When the chicken is coated, sprinkle with salt and pepper.

Place the baby potatoes around the chicken and drizzle olive oil over them. Squeeze one lemon wedge over the chicken, and then stuff the bird's cavity with the remaining lemon wedges.

Place the chicken into the oven and roast for anywhere from 1 to 1½ hours, until an instant-read thermometer reads 165° when inserted into a thick section of the meat.

Remove the roasting pan from the oven and place the baby potatoes on a cutting board. Smash them, and serve with the chicken.

When you're finished eating, prepare the remaining chicken for additional meals. Pull all of the meat off the chicken's bones, and discard the skin. Dice the remaining meat, store in a container with a lid, and refrigerate.

CHICKEN, SPINACH, AND MUSHROOM RISOTTO

Yes, this one requires constant attention.
But your diligence will be rewarded.

ACTIVE TIME 30 MINUTES

Ingredients

½ cup chicken, diced

½ cup baby spinach

½ cup button mushrooms, chopped

2 cups chicken broth

1 tablespoon olive oil

1 tablespoon butter

⅛ cup chopped shallots

1 garlic clove, minced

⅛ cup white wine

Salt to taste

½ cup arborio rice

¼ cup parmesan cheese, grated, plus additional cheese for garnish

Directions

Place the chicken broth in a small saucepan and cook over medium heat until it simmers. Remove from heat and set aside.

Place the olive oil and butter in a medium skillet and cook over medium heat until the butter is melted. Add the shallot and garlic and cook until they are soft. Add mushrooms and chicken, cook for 5 minutes, and then add salt. Stir in the rice and toast it for 3 minutes.

Directions
(continued)

Add the white wine and cook until it is almost absorbed. Add the broth, ¼ cup at a time, until it is completely absorbed. Stir in the parmesan cheese and the spinach. When the spinach has wilted, remove the skillet from the stove, garnish with additional parmesan cheese, and serve.

CHICKEN ENCHILADAS

Corn or flour tortillas work equally well in this recipe. Tortillas often come in handy, and they freeze well, so don't be afraid to stock up.

ACTIVE TIME 20 MINUTES

Ingredients

1 cup chicken, diced

½ cup black beans

½ teaspoon cumin

½ cup salsa, plus more for garnish

½ cup frozen corn, defrosted

¼ cup cheddar cheese, shredded

2 soft corn or flour tortillas

2 tablespoons fresh cilantro, chopped, for garnish

Directions

Preheat oven to 375°.

Grease a small baking dish with cooking spray or olive oil. Add the chicken, black beans, cumin, salsa, and corn to a bowl, stir until combined, and set aside.

Reserve ¼ cup of the bean mixture, and then divide the chicken and bean mixture, and half of the cheese between the two flour tortillas. Roll the tortillas and place them, seam-side down, in the baking dish. Top with the remaining bean mixture, cheese, and some salsa, wrap the dish in foil, and place in the oven for 30 minutes. When enchiladas are done, garnish with the cilantro, and serve.

CHICKEN LETTUCE WRAPS

Snag some lettuce leaves from your salad prep,
and you're more than halfway home.

ACTIVE TIME 20 MINUTES

Ingredients

1 cup chicken, diced

1 tablespoon olive oil

1 garlic clove, minced

1 teaspoon ginger, minced

1 tablespoon rice wine vinegar

1 tablespoon soy sauce

2 tablespoons green onion, chopped

½ cup white rice, cooked

¼ carrot, grated

2 large lettuce leaves (bibb works well)

Directions

Place the olive oil in a frying pan and cook over medium heat until it begins to sizzle. Place the garlic, ginger, and green onion in the frying pan and cook until they begin to soften. Add the chicken, rice wine vinegar, and soy sauce.

When the chicken is heated through, remove pan from the stove. Place the lettuce leaves on a plate, and divide the rice and carrots between them.

Divide the chicken mixture between the leaves, roll them closed, and serve.

CHICKEN FRIED RICE

Chinese takeout, without having to go anywhere.
If you have some vegetables kicking around in the fridge,
this recipe is a good way to use them up.

ACTIVE TIME 20 MINUTES

Ingredients

1 cup chicken, diced

1 tablespoon olive oil

1 garlic clove, minced

½ teaspoon ginger, grated

1 cup chopped vegetables
(Whatever's in the refrigerator!)

1 teaspoon soy sauce

1 cup white or brown rice,
cooked

1 egg

Directions

Add the olive oil, garlic, and ginger to a frying pan and cook over medium-high heat until the garlic is soft. Add the vegetables, cook until soft, and then add the rice, stirring continuously.

Crack the egg into a bowl and whisk until fluffy. Pour the egg into the pan, and stir until it has cooked.

Add soy sauce, salt, and pepper, stir to combine, and serve.

Roasted Pork Loin—Five Meals

ROASTED PORK LOIN

If you don't cook pork much, this recipe
will show you what you've been missing.

ACTIVE TIME 20 MINUTES

Ingredients

1 pork loin, 3 pounds

3 garlic cloves, minced

Salt and pepper to taste

¼ cup olive oil

Directions

Preheat oven to 350° and line a baking dish with parchment paper or aluminum foil. While the oven is heating, pat the pork loin dry with a cotton or paper towel.

Add the garlic, salt, pepper, and olive oil to a bowl and stir until combined into a paste. Slather the pork loin with the paste, place it in the baking dish, and place the dish in the oven. Cook for 1 hour, or until an instant-read thermometer reads 145°.

Remove the pork loin and serve with a small salad or vegetable.

When you are finished eating, cut the remaining pork loin into bite-sized cubes, or shred it, and store in an airtight container in the refrigerator.

ROASTED PORK TACOS WITH AVOCADO AND SALSA VERDE

Quick and delicious. Serve them with extra salsa verde, tortilla chips, and greens.

ACTIVE TIME 15 MINUTES

Ingredients

1 cup pork, shredded

1 tablespoon olive oil

1 garlic clove, minced

½ cup green cabbage, shredded

½ cup avocado, sliced

2 tablespoons cilantro, chopped

¼ cup salsa verde

3 6-inch soft corn tortillas

½ lime

Directions

Place the tortillas in the microwave and cook on high for 15 seconds, so that they are warmed through. Remove from microwave and set aside.

Place the olive oil and the garlic in a frying pan and cook over medium heat until the garlic begins to soften. Add the pork and cook until heated through.

When the pork is ready, divide the contents of the frying pan between the three tortillas. Top with the green cabbage, avocado, salsa verde, and cilantro, squeeze the lime over each taco, and serve.

BARBECUED PORK SANDWICH WITH COLESLAW

Take a trip down South with this quick, hearty sandwich.
Great for lunch or dinner.

ACTIVE TIME 20 MINUTES

Ingredients

1 cup pork, shredded

½ cup barbecue sauce

1 bulkie roll, split in half

1 cup green cabbage, shredded

⅛ teaspoon celery seed

¼ cup carrots, julienned

1 teaspoon apple cider vinegar

¼ cup mayonnaise

Salt and pepper to taste

Directions

Coleslaw:

Place the green cabbage, carrots, celery seed, apple cider vinegar, mayonnaise, salt, and pepper in a bowl, stir to combine, and set aside.

Place the barbecue sauce in a small saucepan and cook over medium heat for 2 minutes. Add the pork and cook until the barbecue sauce is bubbling slightly and the pork is heated through.

Divide the coleslaw between the two halves of the bulkie roll. Top each half with the barbecue pork, and serve.

PORK AND BLACK BEAN QUESADILLA

We prefer this one open-faced instead of the traditional two-tortilla setup, but don't be afraid to experiment.

ACTIVE TIME 20 MINUTES

Ingredients

1 cup pork, diced

2 large flour tortillas

½ cup black beans

⅛ teaspoon cumin

⅛ teaspoon chili powder

Salt and pepper to taste

½ cup cheddar cheese, shredded

1 cup lettuce, shredded

¼ cup sour cream

½ ripe avocado, smashed

Tomato salsa to taste

Pickled jalapeño slices (optional)

2 tablespoons cilantro, chopped, for garnish

Directions

Preheat oven to 375° and line a baking sheet with aluminum foil. Combine the black beans, cumin, and chili powder in a bowl and set aside. Place the tortilla on the baking sheet and spread the pork and black beans over it. Sprinkle the cheddar cheese on top, season with salt and pepper, cover with another tortilla, and then place the baking sheet in the oven. Bake for 15 to 20 minutes, or until cheese begins to bubble and brown.

Remove the sheet from the oven. Top the quesadilla with lettuce, sour cream, the avocado, salsa, and, if desired, pickled jalapeño. Garnish with cilantro and serve.

PORK RAMEN

Yes, Ramen. Believe me, this recipe is a huge improvement on what you survived on during college.

ACTIVE TIME 20 MINUTES

Ingredients

1 cup pork, sliced

2 cups chicken stock

1 tablespoon miso paste

¼ teaspoon fish sauce

1 tablespoon soy sauce

1 teaspoon fresh squeezed lime juice

Noodles from 1 packet of Ramen

¼ bean sprouts

¼ chopped green chives

1 hardboiled egg, halved

2 tablespoons green onions, sliced

Salt and pepper to taste

Drizzle of sesame oil

Directions

Place the chicken stock, fish sauce, lime juice, salt, and pepper in a small saucepan, stir to combine, and cook over medium-high heat. When the mixture is boiling, add the pork and cook until heated through. Add the noodles and cook until they are soft.

Remove the saucepan from heat, whisk in miso paste, and transfer contents to a bowl. Top with green onions and the sesame oil, and serve.

*Umami, which refers to the fifth taste, originates from Japan
and creates a flavor that is unlike sweet, sour, salty, or bitter. It
corresponds with glutamates and miso paste is a key component.*

CHAPTER NINE

Desserts and Snacks

There is nothing more decadent than enjoying a snack or a dessert by yourself. And when you take the time to choose a beautiful glass goblet, or a special plate or bowl, it elevates the experience that much more. So don't settle for a pint of ice cream on the couch—take the time to do it right and turn that treat into an event.

HOMEMADE POTATO CHIPS

Homemade potato chips can accompany a lot of different things, but they also stand alone extremely well. This recipe makes a small bag of chips, enough for a handful of snacks.

ACTIVE TIME 45 MINUTES **MAKES** 4 SERVINGS

Ingredients

2 medium russet potatoes, peeled and thinly sliced

Canola oil for frying

1 tablespoon salt

Directions

Place potatoes into a bowl of ice water. Add salt to the bowl, drain and rinse the potatoes several times, and then let them dry on a paper towel.

Place an inch of oil in a cast iron skillet or Dutch oven and heat until the oil reaches 365°. Add the potatoes in batches and fry until they turn golden brown. When they are golden brown, remove, let them dry on a paper towel, and sprinkle with salt.

When all of the potatoes have been fried and are cool, place the chips in an airtight container.

SPICED NUT MIX

A small bowl of spiced nuts is perfect with a freshly made cocktail. This simple combo can help you outdo your favorite drinking establishment while you wait for your dinner to cook.

ACTIVE TIME 45 MINUTES **MAKES** 4 SERVINGS

Ingredients

1 cup of unsalted nuts (Walnuts, pecans, cashews, and almonds all work well.)

½ teaspoon salt

¼ teaspoon pepper

⅛ teaspoon chili powder

⅛ teaspoon ground cumin

⅛ cup light brown sugar

½ tablespoon butter

2 tablespoons water

Directions

Preheat oven to 350° and line a baking sheet with parchment paper.

Add the nuts, salt, pepper, chili powder, and cumin to a bowl and toss until combined.

Place the brown sugar, butter, and water in a microwave-safe bowl and microwave for approximately 1 minute, or until the butter is melted. Remove from microwave, pour over the nuts, and stir until the nuts are evenly coated.

Put the nuts on the baking sheet in an even layer and place the sheet into the oven. After 12 minutes, remove the sheet and stir the nuts. Return the sheet to the oven and cook for an additional 5 minutes. Remove sheet from oven and allow to cool before serving.

CHOCOLATE-DIPPED PRETZELS

Chocolate-dipped pretzels can fall into the snack category or the dessert category. Whatever you want them to be, make sure to whip them up ahead of time so there's always a handful around.

ACTIVE TIME 20 MINUTES **MAKES** 4 SERVINGS

Ingredients

2 cups of pretzel rods or twists

½ cup bittersweet chocolate chips

Directions

Line a baking sheet with parchment paper.

Place chocolate chips in microwave-safe container and microwave for approximately 1 minute, or until they are melted.

Remove chocolate chips from the microwave and dip the pretzels into the chocolate, so that half of the pretzel is coated. Place the pretzels on baking sheet. If the chocolate starts to harden, return to the microwave for 10 seconds.

When all the pretzels have been coated, place the baking sheet in the refrigerator. Remove after a half-hour and store in an airtight container.

DECADENT HOT CHOCOLATE

Hot chocolate can be enjoyed at any time of day, but this version makes for a perfect dessert. Especially when it's topped with whipped cream and dark chocolate shavings.

ACTIVE TIME 15 MINUTES

Ingredients

1 cup whole milk

2 tablespoons unsweetened cocoa powder

3 tablespoons sugar

Handful of bittersweet or semisweet chocolate chips

Pinch of salt

Whipped cream for garnish

Dark chocolate shavings for garnish

Directions

Add milk, cocoa powder, and sugar to a small saucepan and whisk continuously while cooking over medium heat. When heated through, add chocolate chips and salt, and continue to whisk until the contents of the pan become frothy and begin to simmer. Pour into a warm mug, top with whipped cream and chocolate shavings, and serve.

STRAWBERRIES ROMANOFF

Choose your glassware carefully with this one, as it's worthy of dressing up. It's a nice time to break into your china cabinet and select a crystal goblet or an etched glass bowl.

ACTIVE TIME 20 MINUTES

Ingredients

1 cup whole strawberries, hulled

3 tablespoons Grand Marnier

⅛ cup whipping cream

Sugar to taste

Splash of vanilla extract

Mint leaves for garnish

Directions

Place the strawberries and the Grand Marnier in a bowl. Place the bowl in the refrigerator and chill for 2 to 4 hours.

When strawberries and Grand Marnier are chilled, place the whipping cream, sugar, and vanilla extract in a bowl and whip until stiff peaks begin to form.

Place the strawberries in a crystal goblet. Pour the Grand Marnier over the berries, top with the whipped cream, garnish with the mint leaves, and enjoy.

CHOCOLATE SOUFFLÉ

When you really need a pick-me-up, turn to
the chocolate soufflé. It's worth the effort.

ACTIVE TIME 30 MINUTES

Ingredients

1 tablespoon unsweetened cocoa powder

1½ tablespoons unsalted butter

2 ounces bittersweet chocolate

Splash of vanilla extract

1 tablespoon sugar

Pinch of salt

1 egg, yolk and white separated

Pinch of cream of tartar

Powdered sugar for garnish

Directions

Preheat oven to 375°. Grease an eight-ounce ramekin with butter and then dust it with cocoa powder.

Place the butter and chocolate in a microwave-safe container and microwave for approximately 1 minute, until it is melted and smooth.

Remove bowl from the microwave, add the vanilla extract and egg yolk, and stir until smooth.

Place the sugar, salt, egg white, and cream of tartar in a separate bowl and whisk until stiff (as it's a small amount, you may not see peaks form). Pour this mixture into the chocolate and stir until well-combined.

Pour the mixture into the ramekin and cook until it is puffy, approximately 20 minutes. Remove, garnish with powdered sugar, and enjoy.

COOKIE FOR ONE

Sometimes, it's nice to not have too many cookies around. This recipe makes just enough to enjoy with a cup of tea or a scoop of ice cream.

ACTIVE TIME 30 MINUTES

Ingredients

3 tablespoons brown sugar

2 tablespoons softened butter

Pinch of salt

1 tablespoon egg, beaten

¼ teaspoon vanilla extract

⅓ cup all-purpose flour

⅛ teaspoon baking soda

¼ cup chocolate chips

Sea salt for garnish

Directions

Preheat oven to 350° and line a baking sheet with parchment paper.

Place the brown sugar, butter, salt, egg, vanilla extract, flour, and baking soda in a mixing bowl and stir until combined. Add the chocolate chips and stir until combined. Form the dough into a ball, place on the baking sheet, and flatten into a disc.

Place the baking sheet into the oven and bake for 10 to 12 minutes, until the cookie is golden brown. Remove from the oven, sprinkle with sea salt, and allow to cool before enjoying.

BANANA MUFFINS

These muffins are a great breakfast or snack, and they freeze well, so don't worry about them turning stale.

ACTIVE TIME 30 MINUTES **MAKES** 6 MUFFINS

Ingredients

½ cup light brown sugar

2 ripe bananas

6 tablespoons vegetable oil

1 large egg

½ teaspoon vanilla extract

1 cup all-purpose flour

1 teaspoon baking soda

¼ teaspoon salt

¼ cup cashews

Directions

Preheat oven to 350° and grease six slots of a muffin tin.

Use an electric mixer to beat the brown sugar and bananas until the mixture is fluffy. Add the oil, egg, and vanilla extract and continue to beat until combined. Add the flour, baking soda, salt, and cashews, and beat until smooth. Divide the batter into the greased slots of the muffin tin, filling each cup ¾ of the way.

Place the tin in the oven and bake for 20 minutes, or until a toothpick stuck into the middle of a muffin comes out clean. Remove from the oven, allow to cool, and enjoy.

GRANOLA BARS

Don't get stuck relying on store-bought granola bars—these will be fresher and less sugary.

ACTIVE TIME 45 MINUTES **MAKES** 6 BARS

Ingredients

1 cup rolled oats

½ cup cashews, unsalted

1 tablespoon chia seeds

¼ cup pumpkin seeds

½ cup raisins

2 tablespoons unsalted butter

2 tablespoons honey

2 tablespoons dark brown sugar

¼ teaspoon vanilla extract

Directions

Grease a pie plate and set aside.

Add the oats, cashews, chia seeds, pumpkin seeds, and raisins to a bowl, stir to combine, and set aside.

Add the butter, honey, brown sugar, and vanilla extract to a small saucepan and cook over medium heat until the mixture begins to bubble. Pour the contents of the pan over the oat-and-cashew mixture and stir until the contents of the bowl are evenly coated.

Pour the contents of the bowl into the greased pie plate and press to an even layer that is a ½-inch thick. Place in the refrigerator and chill for 2 hours. Remove and slice into bars.

CHOCOLATE BANANA PUDDING

Banana pudding is comfort food, so break this one out when you're in need of some care. And if you're concerned about having an entire box of Nilla wafers around, don't worry, they freeze really well.

ACTIVE TIME 10 MINUTES

Ingredients

½ cup milk

1 teaspoon cornstarch

1 pinch of salt

¼ cup bittersweet chocolate chips

6 Nilla Wafers

½ cup whipped cream

½ banana, sliced

Directions

Add the milk, cornstarch, and salt to a small saucepan and cook over medium heat. When mixture begins to thicken, add the chocolate chips and cook, while stirring occasionally, until chocolate is melted and mixture is thick enough to coat the back of a spoon. Remove from heat and set aside to cool.

Place two Nilla Wafers at the bottom of a glass bowl or small mason jar. Top with a layer of the cooled chocolate mixture and then add a layer of banana slices. Continue to layer until all the materials have been used. Top with whipped cream and enjoy!

CHOCOLATE MOUSSE

It's way less intimidating than it looks. Whip this on those nights where you need a treat but also want to keep it light.

ACTIVE TIME 10 MINUTES

Ingredients

3 ounces semi-sweet chocolate

1 tablespoon butter

1 egg, white and yolk separated

¼ teaspoon cream of tartar

3 tablespoons sugar

¼ cup heavy cream

¼ teaspoon vanilla extract

Almonds, chopped, for garnish

Directions

Place the chocolate and butter in a microwave-safe bowl and microwave for 60 seconds. If chocolate is not completely melted, return to microwave for 10-second increments until it is. Let chocolate cool slightly, add the egg yolk, and whisk until combined. Set aside.

Place the egg white in another bowl and beat until foamy. Add the cream of tartar and beat until soft peaks form. Slowly add in 2 tablespoons of the sugar and continue beating until stiff peaks form. In another bowl, beat the heavy cream until it begins to thicken. Add the remaining sugar and the vanilla and beat until soft peaks form.

Fold the egg white mixture into the chocolate mixture. Fold in the whipped cream, transfer to a dessert dish, cover, and chill in the refrigerator until the mousse has set. When set, garnish with almonds and enjoy.

VANILLA MILKSHAKE

Easy, refreshing, and delicious—it's a classic for a reason.

ACTIVE TIME 5 MINUTES

Ingredients

½ pint vanilla ice cream

2 tablespoons whole milk

⅛ teaspoon sea salt

½ teaspoon vanilla extract

Mint leaves for garnish, optional

Directions

Place all ingredients in a blender and blend until combined. Pour into a tall glass, garnish with mint, if desired, and enjoy.

APPLE CRISP

This makes for the perfect end to an autumn day.

Ingredients

1 small apple, thinly sliced

2 tablespoons brown sugar

2 tablespoons oats

1 ½ tablespoons flour

¼ teaspoon cinnamon

1 teaspoon butter

Directions

Preheat your oven to 350° F.

Place the apple, half of the brown sugar, ½ tablespoon of the flour, and half the cinnamon in a mixing bowl. Stir until the apples are coated and transfer to a small baking dish or ramekin. Place the remaining ingredients in the mixing bowl, stir until combined, and place on top of the apples.

Place in oven and cook until oats are golden brown. Remove, let cool slightly, and enjoy.

CHOCOLATE CAKE

Got a hankering for chocolate cake? Thanks to
this recipe, a fix is right around the corner.

ACTIVE TIME 5 MINUTES

Ingredients

2½ teaspoons cocoa powder

1½ tablespoons flour

Pinch of salt

2½ teaspoons sugar

⅛ teaspoon baking powder

1½ teaspoons vegetable oil

1½ tablespoons milk

¼ teaspoon vanilla extract

Strawberries, sliced, for garnish

Mint leaf for garnish

Directions

Preheat oven to 350° F.

Place the cocoa powder, flour, salt, sugar, and baking powder
in a mixing bowl and stir until thoroughly combined. Add the
vegetable oil, milk, and vanilla extract and stir to combine.

Grease a ramekin and then place the cake batter into it. Place
the ramekin in the oven and bake for 13 to 14 minutes, or until a
toothpick inserted into the cake comes out clean. Remove, let cool
slightly, garnish with strawberries and the mint leaf, and enjoy.

INDEX

ABOUT THE AUTHOR

Kimberly Stevens is a seasoned writer and journalist who has contributed extensively to *The New York Times* and written stories for *The Los Angeles Times, The Wall Street Journal,* numerous national magazines, and online publications. Her spare time finds her battling a severe addiction to cookbook collecting, shopping at the farmer's market, and making meals for friends and family.

ABOUT CIDER MILL PRESS
BOOK PUBLISHERS

Good ideas ripen with time. From seed to harvest, Cider Mill Press brings fine reading, information, and entertainment together between the covers of its creatively crafted books. Our Cider Mill bears fruit twice a year, publishing a new crop of titles each spring and fall.

CIDER MILL
PRESS

BOOK
PUBLISHERS
KENNEBUNKPORT, MAINE

"Where Good Books Are Ready for Press"

Visit us online at
cidermillpress.com
or write to us at
PO Box 454
12 Spring Street
Kennebunkport, Maine 04046